# Writtle

## College Library

TEL: (01245) 420705

This book must be returned on or before the last date below, otherwise fines will be charged.
Books can normally be renewed unless reserved by another reader.

# ALLEN BREED SERIES

The Allen Breed Series examines horse and pony breeds from all over the world, using a broad interpretation of what a breed is: whether created by the environment where it originally developed, or by man for a particular purpose, selected for its useful characteristics, or for its appearance, such as colour. It includes all members of the horse family, and breeds with closed or protected stud books as well as breeds and types still developing.

Each book in the Allen Breed Series examines the history and development of the breed, its characteristics and use, and its current position in Britain, together with an overview of the breed in America and worldwide. More difficult issues are also tackled, such as particular problems associated with the breed, and such controversies as the effect of the show ring on working breeds. The breed societies and their role in modern breeding policies are discussed.

### BOOKS IN THE SERIES

*The Appaloosa*
*The Arabian Horse*
*The Fell Pony*
*The Hanoverian*
*The Irish Draught Horse*
*The Mule*
*The Quarter Horse*
*The Trakehner*
*The Welsh Mountain Pony*

# The Welsh Mountain Pony

The author with Welsh Mountain pony mare and foal at his Ceulan Stud.

ALLEN BREED SERIES

# The Welsh Mountain Pony

## Wynne Davies

J. A. Allen
London

British Library Cataloguing-in-Publication Data
A catalogue record for this book is available from the British Library

ISBN 0–85131–571–2

Published in Great Britain in 1993 by
J. A. Allen & Company Limited
1 Lower Grosvenor Place, London SW1W 0EL

Series editor Elizabeth O'Beirne-Ranelagh
Book production Bill Ireson
Printed in Great Britain by The Longdunn Press Ltd, Bristol

# Contents

*Front cover:* Ceulan Springson, bred by the author, Mountain and Moorland Supreme Champion at Salisbury and South Wiltshire Show, 1991. (*Photo: Wynne Davies*)

*Endpapers:* Welsh Mountain ponies on the hills. 'Repose', J. F. Herring, 1854. (*Arthur Ackermann & Son Ltd*)

# Preface

I have been breeding Welsh Mountain ponies at Ceulan, Miskin in South Wales since 1960; however, the Ceulan stud is much older than this and has been producing Welsh Mountain ponies since Aeronwen Ceulan was foaled in 1905. Many of the present-day Ceulan ponies trace back directly to this foundation mare. Nineteen foals were born at Ceulan in 1992.

During the early stages of this book, I prepared material on about 40 studs, and I am grateful to the many members of the Welsh Pony and Cob Society with connections to present and past studs for their invaluable assistance. However, within the confines of this book it was only possible to use a selection of these. I hope in a future publication to be able to include all of this information.

My earlier volume, *Welsh Ponies and Cobs* (J. A. Allen 1980), contains additional photographs of a number of the horses and people mentioned in this book.

I would like to thank the following for providing photographs, information, and checking details: Arthur Ackermann & Son Ltd; Len Davies; Emrys Griffiths; Mrs Desda Hone; Mrs Hope G. Ingersoll; Mrs Sheila Johnson; David Lloyd; Robin Morgan, the late Mrs Nell Pennell; Mrs Teresa Smalley; Mrs Sommerville; Mrs Lynn Spears; Dick Swain; John Thomas; and the Welsh Stud Books. I would like to thank my wife, Ruth, for compiling the index.

WYNNE DAVIES

# 1 Introduction

In the Mesolithic period (c. 8000 BC), Britain was joined on to Ireland and Europe and there were no barriers to the migration of Asiatic and African animals from utmost east to utmost west. It may be, therefore, that the so-called Celtic pony left his home in Central Asia and reached Europe before the arrival of Neolithic man (c. 4000 BC). Some of his species might have remained in Wales, as well as in Connemara and the outer Hebrides where, undoubtedly, he has been found. It is probable that the lands of the west of Britain (Wales) were, from a climatic and altitudinous point of view, not as favourable for the breeding and thriving of such animals as those of the east (England), and the horses would be more 'puny', possibly the source of the word 'pony'.

Julius Caesar, writing of his Gallic wars, referred to the Celtic ponies in terms of unqualified admiration, for their docility and speed as chariot horses, for their activity as riding horses, and for their general superiority all round. Unfortunately he omitted to hand down to posterity any clue as to their height.

In the Welsh laws of Hywel Dda (Hywel the Good) in the tenth century, entitled *Leges Wallicae*, the small ponies were left ominously unmentioned. Was it that they were deemed unworthy of notice, or were similar ideas entertained of the ponies as in a later Tudor period? Henry VIII gained almost as much posthumous notoriety from his attitude towards ponies as he earned by his methods of wifely treatment. Larger 'Cobs', weight-carrying armour bearers, and prancing war horses that 'scent battle afar' reigned supreme in his regal mind and occupied his all-conquering thoughts. The self-supporting little pony on the hill was, in his opinion, but a blot upon creation; in 1535 His Majesty pronounced against them a sentence of annihilation, which fortunately he was not able to carry out due to the mountainous and inaccessible regions of the Principality.

No one will ever know if there were 12-hand Welsh Mountain ponies in existence at the time that Hywel Dda codified an exhaustive set of laws, subsequently approved by the Pope, bearing on the subjects of the description of horses in Wales, their breeding, keeping and selling.

Certainly by the end of the twelfth century there were small 'ponies' on the hills. Baldwin, Archbishop of Canterbury, set out on a tour of Wales in 1188 to recruit soldiers for the crusades, accompanied by Giraldus Cambrensis, Archdeacon of Brecon. After the tour, Giraldus (Gerallt Gymro) wrote his famous *Itinerary through Wales* where he describes the hills as being 'full of ponies'. Certainly there were plenty of small mountain ponies in Wales to justify Henry VIII pronouncing his 'death sentence' upon them in 1535. If there were no small ponies in Wales at the time of Hywel Dda, then 300 years of living on the rugged Welsh hills in near-starvation conditions would certainly have reduced their size by the time of Giraldus Cambrensis, and another 400 years still further by the era of Henry VIII to produce what he described as 'nags of small stature'.

Some farmers kept ponies on the hills to open up paths in the bracken along which sheep could follow and graze. In his book *The Horse*, published in 1851, William Youatt describes 'pony hunting' as a favourite amusement amongst the Welsh farmers of the seventeenth century.

There were certainly plenty of 12-hand ponies on the hills of Wales and the border counties by the end of the nineteenth century, as described in the 'roundup' report in the local press on 23 September 1892, when over 1,250 ponies from the Longmynd hills were driven through the main streets of Church Stretton on the Welsh borders.

# 2 Origins and registration of Welsh Mountain ponies

The numbers of ponies (1,000 to 1,500) recorded on the Longmynd hills in 1892 can be multiplied by at least 10 to cover the Brecon Beacons, Eppynt and Carmarthen Van mountains, the Denbigh moors and Gower Common. It is surprising that such large numbers of ponies found a ready market. Many would be sold as pit ponies, others went as smart harness ponies to the large English cities or as riding ponies for the children of wealthy aristocrats. This 'gene pool' of healthy, intelligent mountain ponies of excellent conformation, by judicious breeding over the next century, has provided the present-day Welsh Mountain pony, which can be described, without fear of contradiction, as 'the most beautiful pony in the world'.

To survive the ravages of the weather, and the persecution initiated by Henry VIII's law, a very hardy type of pony developed on the hills of Wales. They were ponies with plenty of bone, mane, tail and feather, of dark colours, the blacks, browns and dark duns (indigenous colours) being the most hardy.

In the nineteenth century, many attempts were made to 'glamorise' the sturdy or 'cobby' type of hill pony by wealthy, well-meaning landowners. Mr Richard

Typical Welsh pony of 'cobby' type, c. 1850. Artist unknown. (*Wynne Davies collection*)

Child on grey pony, Edward Mumphries of Chirbury, 1823. (*Arthur Ackermann & Son Ltd*)

Crawshay Bailey, ironmaster of Merthyr Tydfil, turned out an Arab stallion (sire of the influential Cob stallion Cymro Llwyd) on the hills bordering Merthyr Tydfil and the Brecon Beacons. Lord Oxford owned the Clive Arabian, and Sir Watkin Williams Wynn turned out the English 'Thoroughbred' Merlin (a direct descendant of the Byerly Turk, imported in 1689) on the Ruabon hills in North Wales. Colonel Vaughan of Rug, near Corwen, owned a half-Arab stallion named Apricot which ran out on the hills there. A chestnut standing about 13 hands he was only once beaten on the racecourse by an animal of his own height, which he beat the following year. Mr Williams of Aberpergwm (ancestor of the Williamses of Miskin Manor and Llanharan House) kept a grey Arab stallion which ran out with the local mares behind Aberpergwm around 1840. It was possibly a descendant of this Arab which produced Dyoll Moonlight (dam of the 'Abraham' of the Welsh Mountain pony breed, Dyoll Starlight) in 1886 and introduced the grey colouring into the hill ponies.

Paintings of that period depict the 'improved' type of Welsh Mountain pony showing many of grey colour. A description of the Welsh Mountain pony of the last

'Alarm', J. F. Herring, 1854. Collections J. J. Quelch, Mr and Mrs J. B. Sumner. (*Arthur Ackermann & Son Ltd*)

century, published in the Welsh Stud Book of 1904, was written by the late Sir Richard Green Price, who had made them a life-long study:

> Wonder indeed we may at the survival of these little animals in such a perfect state as we find them today on their native pastures. Persecuted as they have been, not only by laws, but also by the usages of civilisation by their would-be friends, the farmers; by starvation, dog-driving, contaminated by gross carelessness in their mating. In-bred, ill-fed, ill-used and ill-mated for centuries, yet there they are today the living personification of the survival of the fittest, the same little native animals that can live their life where sheep and cattle can only die, with every instinct sharpened by self-preservation, and every limb tested by exertion, they fight their battles unaided, though often in restricted pastures and wired-in mountain enclosures.

To write about the ponies or indeed care about them in the nineteenth century was a very rare occurrence, but even then they were travelling far beyond the hills of Wales. Welsh ponies and Cobs were building up a world-wide reputation in view of their beauty and usefulness. The earliest record of a Welsh pony in Australia, for example, was a five-year-old stallion which was advertised for sale by auction in Sydney on 18 July 1839. A method was needed for identifying the breeding of such ponies. From 1884, the parentage of Welsh breeds could be recorded in the Hackney Stud Book, and from 1894 in the Polo Pony Stud Book as well. But by 25 April 1901, it was decided by ten breeders who met at Llandrindod Wells that the breeds warranted a society and a stud book of their own.

A Welsh Pony and Cob Society of 248 members was formed in 1901 under the presidency of Lord Tredegar. Volume 1 of the Welsh Stud Book, issued in 1902, contained the records of 38 stallions and 571 mares divided into the following sections:

Section A: Welsh Mountain pony under 12 hands 2 in.
Section B: Welsh pony of Cob type under 13 hands 2 in.
Section C: Welsh Cob under 14 hands 2 in.
Section D: Welsh Cob over 14 hands 2 in.

Of the 38 stallions registered in the four sections in Volume 1, 20 were of the hardy black, brown or bay colours, 14 were dark chestnuts, 3 were roans and only one was

6

grey (Dyoll Starlight). There were more greys amongst the mares (mainly in Sections A and B rather than the Cobs), the 571 mares being made up of 367 blacks, browns or bays, 109 chestnuts, 40 roans, 34 greys and 21 duns or creams.

Mr Charles Coltman Rogers, vice-president of the Welsh Pony and Cob Society in 1903, drew attention in 1910 to the 'Cob-type' and 'Arab-type' of Welsh Mountain pony, using as his examples Cream of Eppynt (Cob-type) and Dyoll Starlight (Arab-type). Cream of Eppynt obviously derived his 'Cob type' from his ancestry, since he was sired by the 12 hands 3 in. Gwesyn Flyer (who afterwards for some unknown and perplexing reason had his name changed to 'Llew Llwyd' and became a very influential sire under his new name), who was sired by Trotting Flyer. This

Cream of Eppynt (by Gwesyn Flyer out of Jolly). An example of a Welsh Mountain pony of Cob-type, chosen by Charles Coltman Rogers.

Dyoll Starlight (by Glasallt out of Dyoll Moonlight). Charles Coltman Rogers chose him as an example of the Arab-type of Welsh Mountain pony. (*Photo courtesy of Rosemary Archer*)

14 hands 2 in. Welsh Cob left the best produce around Breconshire of any son of the Old Welsh Flyer (14 hands 3 in., foaled in 1861). Cream of Eppynt himself was only 11 hands 2 in., thus illustrating the rule which generally applies in breeding that progeny follows the size of the dam rather than the sire. Cream of Eppynt's dam was a mare called Jolly from an acknowledged good strain of ponies bred near Abergwesyn.

Dyoll Starlight's sire, grandsire and great-grandsire were respectively Glasallt (12 hands 2 in.), Flower of Wales (12 hands) and Charlie (12 hands 2 in.). Dyoll Starlight owed his sand-born appearance and also his pre-eminence and exceptional attractiveness as an epoch-making sire to some distant ancestor of his dam. Possibly the Arab stallion which Mr Williams turned out on the Aberpergwm hills around 1840 had something to do with Dyoll Moonlight, who was born not too far away in 1886. Dyoll Starlight was one of those miracles of merit and prepotency which revolutionised the Welsh Mountain pony breed. He was the 'High Priest' of Welsh Mountain ponydom.

Cream of Eppynt did not have much influence on the pony breeding of his native Wales since he was exported to Mr Anthony Hordern of Milton Park, New South Wales in 1912, and sold on to found the Richardson's Bereen Stud in Australia in 1918. From his photograph Cream of Eppynt did not have as much bone as one would have expected from his Cob ancestry. Possibly Mr Coltman Rogers selected him as an example of 'Cob-type' on account of his spectacular movement.

Up until Volume 7 of the Welsh Stud Book (1908, with 239 of the first stallions and 1,925 mares registered), the Mountain ponies all appeared in Section A with a maximum height of 12 hands 2 in. Starting in Volume 7, Section A was subdivided into part I, under 12 hands (which could not be hogged or docked), and part II, under 12 hands 2 in., where hogging and docking was acceptable. A report of the 1909 Royal Show held at Gloucester stated that Welsh Mountain pony entries were low since docked ponies were not allowed to compete and many of the winners in Wales were docked ponies. Among these were the following early Welsh Mountain ponies which showed distinctly 'Cobby' characteristics.

Eiddwen Flyer III (blue roan, 1895, registration number 5) had the honour of standing second to Dyoll Starlight in the Welsh Mountain pony stallion class at the 1901 Royal Show (of England) held in Cardiff, and the Show Journal quotes: 'This was a good class. The second-prize winner Eiddwen Flyer III was of great merit but of rather a stronger character than the winner, Dyoll Starlight.' Eiddwen Flyer III (12 hands 2 in.) was sired by Eiddwen Flyer II (13 hands) by Eiddwen Flyer (14 hands 2 in.) by Old Welsh Flyer (14 hands 3 in. and foaled in 1861). Eiddwen Flyer III's dam was a mare by Cymro Llwyd, foaled around 1850 and over 14 hands.

Klondyke (chestnut, 1894, registration number 12) was sired by Young Messenger by Eiddwen Flyer II (above), and his dam was Lady Eiddwen who was a daughter of Eiddwen Flyer. Therefore on his breeding Klondyke would have been expected to be over 14 hands also, but he was only 12 hands 2 in. Klondyke had an enormous effect on the Welsh Mountain breed: Criban Socks (foaled in 1926 and still taken by the WPCS as the perfect example of the breed for publicity purposes) was sired by Criban Shot, son of Criban Chestnut Swell by Ystrad Klondyke by Klondyke. Coed Coch Glyndwr, who had the same effect on the breed in the last 50 years as Dyoll Starlight had 90 years ago, was a son of Dinarth Henol by Llwyn Satan, son of Llwyn Tempter by Temptation by Total by Klondyke. Temptation was exported to the USA in 1915 and Total was exported earlier to New Zealand.

Klondyke. He stood at the Forest Stud, the largest stud at the time, and had a big influence on the breed.

The pedigree of Dick Hill (brown, 1897, registration number 49, 12 hands 2 in.) shows him to be another stallion full of Welsh Cob blood. Dick Hill was the first premium stallion of the Gower Pony Improvement Society, and we shall meet him again in chapter 3 (*p. 27*).

Prince of Cardiff (chestnut, 1895, registration number 84) was bred by James Howell (of the largest store – still carrying his name – in Cardiff). He stood 12 hands 1½ in. and was sired by the Hackney, Hamlet Prince of Denmark, out of the Welsh mare Welsh Wonder (13 hands) by Welsh Flyer (14 hands 3 in.). Prince of Cardiff was purchased by Mr Murless of Plaspower, Wrexham in 1901 for whom he won first prizes at the Welsh National Shows in 1901 and 1902. He also won the WPCS medal at the 1904 Denbigh and Flint Show and was champion at Oswestry in 1903, 1904 and 1905. Prince of Cardiff was brought by Mr Arthur Pughe of the Gwyndy Stud in 1907 and had a big influence on the Gwyndy ponies. However, his greatest

Dick Hill, by Iron Spot, largely of Welsh Cob blood, out of a Welsh Mountain pony mare.

Prince of Cardiff, by a Hackney stallion out of a Welsh mare, was influential through Coed Coch Glyndwr.

mark on the Welsh Mountain pony breed was from his time at Plaspower, where he sired Llwyn Tyrant (grandsire of the illustrious Coed Coch Glyndwr) in 1905.

Titw (chestnut, 1897, registration number 1049), although only 11 hands 3 in. high, was also docked. She was the Mountain pony show mare for John Jones and Son's Dinarth Hall Stud around the turn of the century. Among her more important winnings were (1903): first prize at the Bath and West, first and WPCS medal at Shropshire and West Midland, and first and champion at the Royal of England.

Seren Ceulan (grey, 1910, registration number 5553) stood 12 hands 2 in. Her descendants have had a lasting influence on Welsh Mountain pony premium stallion societies. Her grandson Ceulan Revelry, premium stallion on the Gower, was grandsire of the 1975 Royal Welsh Show winner of the Mountain pony broodmare class, Bryn Ladybird, and the champion Welsh pony of Cob-type, Cefn Moonlight. Another Revelry daughter, Cefn Graceful, is granddam of the famous Section B stallion, Keston Royal Occasion.

**COED COCH GLYNDWR**

| | | | | |
|---|---|---|---|---|
| **Revolt 493** | Llwyn Tyrant 207 | Prince of Cardiff 84 | Hamlet Prince of Denmark 4804, H.S.B. | Robert Elsmere 2659 H.S.B. by Danegelt 174 H.S.B. Allison No. 2, Inspected FS, H.S.B. Vol. 6 Welsh Flyer 856 H.S.B. |
| | | | Welsh Wonder | |
| | | Florence | Eiddwen Flyer III 5 | Eiddwen Flyer II 10 |
| | 145 Llwyn Flyaway | Eiddwen Flyer I 421 | Welsh Flyer 856 H.S.B. | Trotting Comet 834 H.S.B. Trotting Nancy by Cymro Llwyd Welsh Jack by Cymro Llwyd |
| | | | A Pony Mare | |
| | | Llwyn Blaze | | |
| **8683 Dinarth Henol** | Llwyn Satan 1325 | Kilhendre Celtic Silverlight 953 | Bleddfa Shooting Star 73 | Dyoll Starlight 4 572 Alveston Belle by Cymro |
| | | | 4421 Grove Apricot | Stretton Torchlight 123 by Dyoll Starlight Glyn Dolly |
| | | 6086 Llwyn Tempter | Temptation 527 | Total 320 by Klondyke 12 Lady Goldyke by Klondyke 12 |
| | | | 2902 Lady Lightfoot | Gwyndy Cymro 154 Roan Mare by Winnal George |
| | 6350 Irfon Marvel | Dyoll Starlight 4 | Dyoll Glasallt 438 | Flower of Wales |
| | | | 908 Moonlight | |
| | | 3502 Henallt Black | WMP | |
| | | | WMP | |

Pedigree of Coed Coch Glyndwr (foaled 1935, died 1959), showing the influence of the listed stallions.

Titw. A mare of unregistered parentage, she was a championship winner at major shows at the turn of the century.

A notice of motion by Mr H. D. Greene, KC, of the Grove Stud, to limit the Welsh Mountain pony to 12 hands was on the agenda of the Annual General Meeting of the Welsh Pony and Cob Society at Welshpool in September 1909. The sub-division into parts I and II had only taken place the previous year and, although several prominent members spoke in favour of the motion (which would have meant that the most successful stallion Greylight, who grew to just over 12 hands, would not be allowed to compete), it was decided to leave matters as they were. This situation remained until Volume 30 (1931–4), when part II was abandoned and the maximum height of 12 hands was imposed.

It is remarkable how many people think that this 12-hand height limit is a purely arbitrary one which has been imposed by the Welsh Pony and Cob Society without rhyme or reason. In fact it is nothing of the kind, but is insisted upon because long experience has proved conclusively that ponies of this height and less are best able to endure the hardships which they have to face on the Welsh hills throughout the dreary winter months and in the early spring when keep is short and stormy weather is, too frequently, the order of the day. It will thus be seen that the 12-hand maximum is prescribed by nature for the hill-roaming herds, and lowland and overseas breeders from time to time draw re-invigorating blood from hill herds. Size and height in horseflesh, though so frequently confounded, are entirely different criteria and a typical Welsh Mountain pony must be a big one for its inches, that is, a big one in small compass.

An attempt was made at the 1911 Annual General Meeting of members to keep Section A (still parts I and II) self-contained and not to allow in progeny of animals registered in Sections B, C and D. An Extraordinary General Meeting was convened at Llandrindod on 18 October 1911 to discuss the matter further; however, in view of the low numbers of animals registered, it was not passed. For the same reason a motion not to register animals unless both parents were registered was not passed, but the intention to apply this regulation as soon as numbers justified was recorded. Had this regulation been passed in 1911 then the originators of the present-day Section B – for example, Tanybwlch Berwyn (foaled in 1924, sired by the Barb stallion Sahara) and Craven Cyrus (foaled in 1927, sired by the Arab stallion King Cyrus) – would not have been allowed into the Stud Book. One decision made at Llandrindod was not to allow Hackneys into Section C (Welsh Cobs under 14 hands 2 in.) or Section D (Welsh Cobs over 14 hands 2 in.), since many pure Hackneys were winning WPCS medals and competing for (and sometimes winning) the George Prince of Wales Cup at the Welsh National (now the Royal Welsh) Show.

When the Stud Book was restricted to only animals of registered parentage (Volume 29: 1930), again registrations had reached a desperately low ebb and the Foundation Stock scheme was opened. This was for non-registered mares on inspection, whose progeny (FS1 and FS2) by registered sires, again after inspection, would produce registerable stock.

By 1950 there were sufficient Section A animals registered annually to make the section self-contained, and by 1960 there was sufficient breeding stock within the Stud Book to close it to further FS registrations. The tables show the registration figures which were responsible for those decisions.

It is interesting to note registrations peaking to coincide with export booms, e.g. the exports to the USA, Canada and Australia around 1911 and to the Continent around 1965 (1,044 Section A mares were exported to Holland alone in 1965).

The Foundation Stock appendix to the Stud Book served a very useful purpose,

14

Welsh Mountain ponies registered in the Welsh Stud Book, 1902–65

| Volume no. | Date of publication | Stallions | Mares |
|---|---|---|---|
| 1 | 1902 | 9 | 273 |
| 2 | 1903 | 9 | 155 |
| 3 | 1904 | 17 | 133 |
| 4 | 1905 | 6 | 105 |
| 7 | 1908 | 15 | 139 |
| 10 | 1911 | 37 | 394 |
| 15 | 1916 | 19 | 110 |
| 20 | 1921 | 45 | 103 |
| 25 | 1926 | 38 | 94 |
| 28 | 1929 | 26 | 32 |
| 29 | 1930 | 17 | 48 |
| 39 | 1956 | 75 | 228 |
| 49 | 1965 | 712 | 3504* |

* including 1219 FS1 and FS2.

Total registrations in all four sections of the Welsh Stud Book, 1910–90

| Date | Stallions | Mares | Foundation Stock mares |
|---|---|---|---|
| 1910 | 381 | 2,686 | – |
| 1920 | 1,022 | 6,550 | – |
| 1930 | 1,501 | 8,781 | – |
| 1950 | 2,059 | 9,905 | 798 |
| 1960 | 3,437 | 13,479 | 7,489 |
| 1970 | 8,879 | 29,607 | 14,829 |
| 1980 | 22,379 | 68,146 | 17,933 |
| 1990 | 34,720 | 90,000 | 18,204 |

especially after the war, in getting back into the Stud Book (after three generations of top crosses of pure Welsh blood) animals whose registrations had lapsed during the war years and the depression just before it. In WSB Volume 49 (1965), 1,607 of the total females (4,705) registered across Sections A, B, C and D, or 34 per cent, were FS1 and FS2. By 1991 (Volume 72) obviously the original FS mares have long since died or, at least, gone past breeding age, and only seven FS2 fillies were registered from a total of 1,169 (0.6 per cent). Of these 1,607 appendix mares registered in Volume 49, 1,219 (76 per cent) were Section A, 310 (19 per cent) were Section B, 49 (3 per cent) were Section C and 26 (1.6 per cent) were Section D. Approximately the same percentages held true for the fully registered mares. By Volume 72 (1991) the percentages had altered considerably, with the greatest increase being amongst the Cobs. Of 1,162 fully registered mares, only 432 (37 per cent) were Section A.

When the WPCS started in 1901 there were just over 200 members, and this figure remained fairly constant (varying from approximately 150 to 300) until 1953. It increased to 1,230 in 1959; 2,010 in 1963; 3,595 in 1964; 5,572 in 1972 and 6,670 in 1990. The earliest record of a WPCS AGM which I have been able to trace is that for 1907, and it is interesting to compare the £332 turnover with the 1990 figure of £279,304.

The description of the Welsh Mountain pony was laid down in 1908 by Mr John Hill, Church Stretton; Mr H. Meuric Lloyd, Llanwrda; and Mr C. Coltman Rogers, Stanage Park, Radnorshire:

GENERAL CHARACTER: Hardy, spirited and pony-like.

COLOUR: Any colour.

HEAD: Small, clean-cut, well set on, wide between eyes and tapering to muzzle.

EARS: Well placed, small and pointed, well up on the head, proportionately close, not lop-eared.

NOSTRILS: Prominent and open.

THROAT AND JAWS: Finely cut.

NECK: Fairly lengthy and moderately lean with a stronger crest in the case of stallions.

SHOULDER: Long and sloping well back, fine at the points with a deep girth.

FORELEGS: Set square and true, not too far back under the body and not in at the elbows. Long strong forearm, well-developed knee, short flat bone below the knee, pasterns of proportionate slope and length, feet well shaped and round, hoof dense.

BACK AND LOINS: Muscular, strong and short coupled.

HIND QUARTERS: Lengthy and fine, not cobby, ragged or goose-rumped, tail well set on and carried gaily.

HOCKS: Wide, large and clean, parallel with the body and well let down shank and vertical. Neither sickle-hocked nor unduly straight. Adequately bent with long heel or calcis bone. Pasterns of proportionate slope and length, feet well shaped and round, hoof dense.

ACTION: Quick, free and straight from the shoulder, knees and hocks well flexed with straight and powerful leverage well under the body as to the hocks, but with such bending of the knees and hocks as will not sacrifice pace and power.

In accordance with the decision of the 1907 AGM at Llandrindod:

> All such ponies shall show or their owners be able to prove unquestioned descent on one side or the other and not further back than the grandsire and granddam from animals that were foaled or have run wild on the Mountains or Moorlands of Wales or scheduled portions of the Border Counties, or are descendants of ponies already entered in Section A of the Welsh Stud Book.

Despite the enormous scientific discoveries of this century, including grassland improvement, easy transport (e.g. of mares to stallions), artificial insemination, embryo transfer and so on, the above description has not altered greatly over 80 years, apart from colour which must not be piebald or skewbald.

Mr Coltman Rogers had written in 1909 of the 'Cob-type' and 'Arab-type' of Welsh Mountain pony; 80 years later we still have the same diversity of type, and who is to dictate which is the 'right' type or the 'wrong' type? Both types conform to the description laid down in the Stud Book and it is up to the breeder to breed whichever type he pleases!

To illustrate the divergence of types I have selected two consecutive Royal Welsh Show champions (1955 and 1956): Coed Coch Siaradus and Brierwood Honey. They were adjudged by two senior members of the Welsh Pony and Cob Society: my father, Mr E. S. Davies, who joined the society in 1915, and Mrs Nell Pennell, member since 1919.

Coed Coch Siaradus (foaled in 1942) had a neat head, a long lean neck with a superb sloping shoulder, which meant that she could move at a fair pace, a short strong back with well-defined croup, a well-set tail, good hind-quarters, and good limbs without too much bone but no feather. Brierwood Honey (foaled in 1947) had an elegant head with huge eyes and minute ears. She had abundant bone and feather, but a short thick neck, a rounded croup, and she moved with very short steps.

Between 1956 and the present day one can also classify the subsequent cham-

Coed Coch Siaradus, a Royal Welsh Show champion of the 'slight' type.

18

Brierwood Honey, a Royal Welsh Show champion of the 'heavy' type.

pions into these two extreme types with various 'intermediate' examples, and the same variation of types can be found within the Welsh ponies, Welsh ponies of Cob-type, and the Welsh Cobs.

# 3   Improvement schemes

## The Commons Act

An important milestone in the development of the native Welsh Mountain pony was the passing of the Commons Act 1908 (8 Ed. 7 c. 44) to regulate the turning out upon Commons of entire animals. The campaign of the Welsh Pony and Cob Society Council with the Board of Agriculture had taken almost seven years, but Council reported in 1908:

> The legislators have given what was asked, the hill clearers have got what they besought. We have, in short, obtained what we clamoured for, which was nothing more or less than an Act of Parliament, which if taken due advantage of, may be found productive of much utility to that subordinate agricultural industry of Wales, pony breeding on the hills and commons.

Greatest thanks for this success were due to the Minister of Agriculture, Lord Carrington, who steered the Bill through the shoals and eddies of our parliamentary procedure – a Bill, moreover, of rather an inglorious character that, after all, concerned but a few and appealed to still fewer. Support in the House of Lords was received from Lords Kenyon, Powis, Cawdor, Tredegar and Plymouth, who were former presidents of the WPCS. Lord Kenyon had previously advocated the regulating of stallions in his report to the Welsh Land Commission Enquiry in 1894.

Breeders in Wales were urged to put the principles of the Commons Act into operation to keep up and improve their naturally excellent pony product. 'Where those principles have been put into operation, and where promiscuity with its mixture of Sires and medley of Mares has ceased, there will the buyer wend his way.' By 1910 the Church Stretton hills and the Gower Common had implemented the Act, and they reaped the benefit when the Americans purchased Mountain ponies in large numbers in 1912.

Church Stretton strictly speaking was outside the Principality but, for many years, their ponies had been intermixed with Welsh ponies from over the border and were regarded as an identical race. Among the eight approved Church Stretton stallions in 1909 were two sons of Dyoll Starlight: Dyoll Radium and Brigand (the latter exported to the USA in 1912). Church Stretton members rounded up, selected, eliminated and changed sires which had served their time. Those that were better elsewhere were firmly dealt with. Their hills were becoming free from carelessly bred nondescripts and soon abounded in uniform mobs of typically fixed animals, the best instead of the worst that the hills could produce.

Gower Common was the next to implement the Act under the energetic auspices of the Hon. Odo Vivian (later to be Lord Swansea).

The effect of the Act as viewed by outsiders can be appreciated by quoting from a privately printed booklet by American Olive Tilford Dargan:

> The Common Lands of Wales are so extensive and comprise so many tracts that improvement by selection other than nature's is a farce as long as the pasturage is free to any and all. Nature long ago accomplished her best for the Welsh pony, and while he was practically an isolated type, it was easy to maintain his standard. But with multifarious breeds and half-breeds in proximity, the carelessness of man was beginning to undo her work, and Wales might have followed Ireland in the deterioration of her pony stock and the loss of a fixed type, if the Society had not intervened. The struggle over the Act was discouragingly prolonged for Taffy is sometimes stubborn and he could not see that the right to use the Commons would still be a right if it were limited by consideration for one's neighbours. His beast might be as poor a thing as he pleased – sickle-hocked, goose-rumped, tucked up in the brisket as some of the larger valley-bred ponies were, and alas, are – but if it could successfully beguile the feminine portion of his neighbour's carefully sorted drove, the helpless neighbour, injured in heart and pocket, had no redress. Finally, after many difficulties, unwearying effort and a constant display of good nature, the committee secured the passage of the Act and put an end to what one of the overworked members, exasperated to humour, termed the 'unlimited liability sire system'.

On 10 February 1912 the President of the Board of Agriculture appointed a committee to advise him on the improvement of Mountain and Moorland ponies, with Mr Coltman Rogers representing the Welsh Pony and Cob Society and Lord Arthur Cecil as Chairman. The report produced by this committee made the following points:

(i) The work which the ponies carry out was referred to. The Mountain ponies

Criban (R) mares and foals running on Blaentaff hills in the Brecon Beacons.

were originally used as saddle ponies, but later they were used increasingly as pit ponies, pack ponies (e.g. bundles of peat or baskets of farm produce), and the ideal draft horse for the smallholder, being able to shift a considerable load at a fair pace.

(ii) Many famous Thoroughbred racehorses were quoted which had native ponies in their pedigrees.

(iii) 'Nimrod', in a series of articles about his hunters, quoted that they had been purchased on the borders of Wales and were of Welsh pony extraction. These are the hunters which come out in their turn without fail, which jog home cheerfully after a hard run, cleaning out their mangers to the last oat. Some Grand National winners with native pony ancestors were quoted.

(iv) Welsh ponies had been influential in the development of Hackneys and Polo Ponies.

The report continued with an interesting survey of the native pony breeds in Britain at that time, and their premium schemes:

(i) Dartmoor: 33 stallions purchased by the improvement societies for £15 each and each awarded a premium of £7 to run with about 35 mares each.

(ii) Exmoor: six stallions purchased and given premiums of £5 each.

(iii) New Forest: over 100 stallions are shown annually and £150 distributed in premiums.

(iv) Fell and Highland: nine premiums of £5 awarded to Highland stallions. Six premiums of £20 each awarded to Fell stallions.

(v) Welsh: Church Stretton (8 premiums of £5) to be selected on 25 April; Eppynt (9 premiums of £5); Gower (3 premiums of £5); and Penybont (3 premiums of £5). Before the premium was paid the stallion had to be registered with the Welsh Pony and Cob Society. The selection judges had to be appointed by the Board of Agriculture and the stallions would have to run out at large on the mountains from 1 May to 1 August. They should only serve mares registered or accepted for entry in the Welsh Stud Book.

As a result of government support given in the report, it became apparent that implementation of the 1908 Commons Act brought its rewards to the respective breeders, and other areas were encouraged to form improvement societies.

## Stretton Hill Pony Improvement Society

Even before the formation of 'premium' societies as a result of the 1908 Commons Act, the pony breeders of Church Stretton had already formed their own improvement society, records of which exist back to 1892. In the Church Stretton area, many hundreds of ponies were kept on the Longmynd mountains, rising to over 1,700 feet above sea level on the borders of Wales. The Longmynd range of mountains are part of what was known as the 'Long Mountain Forest' during the reign of King John, and it is recorded in the local history of the area that King John turned out a stallion into this forest 'to improve the local ponies'.

President of the Stretton Hill (Longmynd) Pony Improvement Society in 1892 was Mr J. Hill, JP, of Felhampton Court, who contributed only one shilling membership to the funds! However, the balance sheet shows some very generous donations, such as £15 from W. E. Downing of Stourbridge, which along with about 50 membership fees of one shilling enabled the society to purchase five stallions at £11 to £15 (two of which were sold at the end of the year at £9 and £13).

The society was fortunate in having John Hill as their president. He had written many articles on the Welsh Mountain pony and had been a member of the Editing Committee of the Polo Pony Stud Book Society (now the National Pony Society) since its inception in 1893. Frederick Hill (son of John Hill) of Felhampton Court was the Secretary of the Polo Pony Stud Book Society. The Stretton Hill Society was also fortunate to have the services of local schoolmaster W. J. Roberts, who wrote out the minutes conscientiously in copper-plate handwriting for many years. This task was taken over by his son A. E. (Tommy) Roberts, who loved his ponies right up until his death in 1979 just before his ninetieth birthday.

Of the 1,250 ponies rounded up on 23 September 1892, nine stallions were inspected and the Committee secured the removal of six undesirable stallions. The society sponsored the prize money (£5 for stallions and mares and £2 for colts) at Marshbrook Show that year, and gave £10 for stallions and £7 for mares at the Shropshire and West Midland Show at Knighton. This was very generous prize money, equivalent to about 50 times these figures today.

John Hill described the Church Stretton roundups:

> It was a beautiful sight and a most exciting day's amusement to see the ponies being driven down into the town, besides being productive of untold advantage to all concerned. The establishment of a section for them in the Stud Book, which everybody admits is the foundation of all that is good in Cobs or ponies in Wales, has come none too soon.

He continues: 'I regret to say that for the last few years this excellent system has been dropped in Church Stretton and breeders seem to have lost their enthusiasm.' This was in 1902; fortunately the 'loss of enthusiasm' proved to be only a temporary phase and the minute book shows the society in good heart and the finances in good shape by 1907. By this date the Welsh Pony and Cob Society had been formed, and the Church Stretton Society was given a good boost when a deputation from the WPCS waited on the Minister of Agriculture in 1906 to draw up the Commons Act.

At the Annual Church Stretton Show held on 23 September 1908, over £50 was offered in prize money in 15 classes, followed by a sale by auction. The sale was successful, Mr Puttock buying a stallion from Mr Hamer for £20 and mares selling for up to £16. Dyoll Starlight was paraded (for the benefit of breeders but not for competition) at the 1908 show, for which his owner was sincerely thanked.

The report on one roundup says:

> the roundup was not so successful as usual due to a badly organised start and an insufficient number of horsemen at the lower end of the hill; consequently many ponies were left behind. All the stallions were examined by the Committee, five yearlings and two two-year-olds were condemned and the owners promised to have them castrated or sold out of the district.

A financial problem which worried the Committee was the cost of the keep of their nine stallions for the winter, which amounted to £8! Another disaster which struck in 1908 was that Sirroco (son of Dyoll Starlight), which was their most expensive purchase (£20), broke out in the night, got in amongst some big shod horses, got his hind leg shattered and had to be put down. However, on hearing about this tragedy, the Commoners Association, who had lent £20 to purchase the stallion, gave £9 'donation' to alleviate some of the loss!

The annual roundups were reported in detail in the local press. The 1909 roundup was thought to be the most successful up to that date:

> About 8 a.m. a number of horsemen assembled at the Hill End, near Plowden, and advanced across the top of the hill. Parties of men on each side of the hills drove the ponies up the valleys to the top in time to meet the horsemen. A semi-circle of horsemen and men was formed, into which the ponies were driven, the numbers increasing as the party advanced across the top to Inwood (All Stretton), when the ponies were driven down the valley to the main road, and brought to Church Stretton. Between 300 and 400 ponies were thus gathered, and a pretty picture they made as they galloped down the street with a cavalcade of horsemen bringing up the rear.

Members of the Welsh Pony and Cob Society were always ready to lend a helping hand to societies such as the Church Stretton Society. For example, at the 1918 judging of premium stallions, along with Mr Carter of the Board of Agriculture (who provided the funding), there was the Secretary of the WPCS (Mr J. Bache), two inspection judges, and Mr Charles Coltman Rogers (WPCS Chairman). Some of the mare owners were getting a little dubious as to the wisdom of using so many stallions of the Dyoll Starlight strain. They thought that a certain infusion of Cob blood, an introduction of larger, bulkier sires, would bring about a better result, because the progeny of a Cob sire would be larger, thicker and stronger, more valuable and more sought-after.

Mr Coltman Rogers disagreed violently with the views of these mare owners. He persuaded them that the produce of Cob or 'Cart' sires might gain in coarser qualities and outward semblance of strength but would lose in shapeliness; also that progeny follow the size of the dam more than the sire and, under the severe environment of the hilltops, soon revert to smaller size. He said that:

> unless you improve the pasturage of the hills by drainage, shelters, manuring or such reclamation process, the ponies will refuse to produce an enlarged type. If your ambition is to breed cheap pit ponies, a cheaper coster barrow and suchlike cart shaft drudges, well then go back to your old system of non-selection and mesalliances and admit that the note of progress has been sounded in vain and that the efforts of improvement are better discarded. But if you want to breed ponies for export, for the boys and girls of wealthy purchasers, then they must be narrow, shapely and easy-actioned, not broad-backed, leg-splitting, bone-shaking miniature Cobs.

Mr Coltman Rogers reminded members of the Church Stretton Society that their 'improved' ponies of 50 years of careful breeding (including 30 years by co-operative breeders before the society was formed) had been good moneyspinners for farmers of that area, many having been sold for export at good prices. The number of ponies sold from Church Stretton for export to America, for example, were in 1909, 31 ponies at an average price of £8 each; in 1910, 61 ponies at £12; and in 1911, 50 ponies at £14.

Fortunately, Mr Coltman Rogers's opinion was held in high esteem, and luckily for present-day breeders, who have often gone to Church Stretton ponies to produce valuable outcrosses to their lowland studs, the stallions were kept pure and the breeding programme zealously guarded.

## Premium stallions

In addition to Church Stretton, local pony improvement societies were set up elsewhere, including the Gower and Eppynt. The Gower Association, formed in 1909, was fortunate in having the patronage of the Hon. Odo Vivian. The following report appeared in the *South Wales Daily Post*:

> A meeting was held at the Gower Inn, Park Mill, on Tuesday night of the recently formed Gower Union Pony Association, Hon. Odo Vivian presiding. This association has been formed for the purpose of improving the breed of the Gower mountain ponies, which has been found to have deteriorated.
>
> A fine stallion pony was produced, and, judging by the remarks passed, gave the utmost satisfaction and a promise of an improved order of things. The pony is entered for the Welsh Pony and Stock Show, and is named 'Dick Hill'. His pedigree is a brilliant one: by Iron Spot, by Trotting Express, King Jack, Wonderful Comet, Comet, and Old Trotting Comet, the sire of Old Welsh Flyer, the progenitors of the Welsh pony breed. 'Dick Hill' hails from Llangammarch.
>
> The service was understood to be limited to members of the association, but Gower farmers can join on payment of 5s, entitling them to one free service.

Eight stallions were awarded premiums for Church Stretton in 1909, and four premiums of £5 each were awarded in 1912, the best two stallions being Dyoll Dynamite and Torchlight, both sired by Dyoll Starlight. Eighteen stallions paraded for premiums at Church Stretton on 23 April 1913, the judges being Mr J. R. Bache, Secretary of the Welsh Pony and Cob Society, and Mr Charles Coltman Rogers, accompanied by Captain Hamilton Pryce and Mr McCall from the Board of Agriculture. The lucrative export trade had given pony breeding a much-required boost and nine stallions were awarded premiums; one stallion with the unfortunate name of Stretton Small Eye, however, was not awarded a premium!

Nine premiums were also awarded at Eppynt that year, the records showing that the inspection was interrupted from time to time by squadrons of mounted Yeomanry from the Eppynt camps, keenly engaged in mimic warfare. The Secretary of the Eppynt Association was Mr J. L. Davies, whose son, grandson and great-great-grandson successfully compete with their ponies at the present day. In order to cover the whole of the 50 miles length and 20 miles breadth of the Eppynt, the premium shows were alternated annually between the Drovers Arms, Merthyr Cynog and Cwmowen.

The Gower Pony Association's Stallion
DICK HILL
Vol II W.C & P.S.B. no 49 Brown 13 hands
foaled 1877

Sire – Iron Spot no 53 WC + PSB
Dam Welsh mountain Pony.
Iron Spot by King Jack HSB 1062, dam by Young Sailor
G.d sire Wonderful Comet by Comet HSB 931
G.d g.d sire Old Trotting Comet HSB 834 the sire
of the renowned Old Welsh Flyer, + the fastest Trotter of his day

Dick Hill as will be seen from the above has
a true pedigree of the best Welsh blood
which can be traced in the WC + PSB for nine generations.
Vol II Welsh Pony Stud Bk in it's history of the
Comets page xliv say " Trotting speed + action,
"on the road were the chief characteristics of
"the Comets (nos 834 + 931)..... the family has
"extended it'self far + wide + great appreciation
"manifested everywhere towards the strain."
Dick Hill's sire + g.d sire are both noted trotters
the g.d sire having been sold for £300.
He is very fast, perfect pony action, has plenty
of bone + substance + great strength, a
thorough hardy mountaineer.

Service limited to members of the Gower Pony
Association. Grooms fee 2/6.
For particulars as to the Society apply to
Mr. W. Kneath Junr. Gellyhir, Three crosses,
who is authorized to receive subscriptions for membership

Odo Vivian
President of the
Gower Pony Association.

The local societies were responsible for:

(i) the turning out of entire animals on the Common;
(ii) the removal of any animal found on the Common in contravention of the regulations;
(iii) the detention and disposal of any animals so removed;
(iv) the raising of expenses incurred in connection with these regulations;
(v) the appointment of officers to enforce the regulations.

On Eppynt, five shillings reward was offered to any shepherd who reported the presence of an unapproved stallion on the Common. The money was raised by inflicting a money penalty on the owner of such an animal, or if the animal was ownerless, it could be sold under the Commons Act to defray expenses.

Some societies bought their own stallions, for around £20 to £30, regaining this sum by charging every member 2 shillings and 6 pence for every mare running on the Common. In order to minimise the selling of filly foals, the products of premium stallions, which would restrict the expansion of improvement brought about by the Government scheme by selling off the goose that would later lay the golden eggs, a money fine was imposed on breeders attempting to sell filly foals at auction.

The Carmarthenshire Black Mountain Pony Society started organising itself in 1912 in order to reap the benefit of the Government premiums, with Mr Edgar Herbert acting as organiser and Secretary. The area was sub-divided into the Brynamman area and the Gwynfe area. In Gwynfe alone on 4 December 1912 almost 100 mares were inspected for registration before darkness set in and the inspections had to be postponed.

Despite the war conditions, by 1916 five societies were well-enough organised to qualify for premiums: Longmynd (Church Stretton), Gower, Carmarthenshire Black Mountains, Penybont (Radnorshire) and Eppynt. The Gower inspection took place at Mr F. Fitch Mason's Fairwood Manor. Altogether 120 mares ran out on the two Commons, Fairwood (about two miles square) and Pengwern (one and

(*Opposite page*) Description of Dick Hill, the Gower Pony Association's first premium stallion, in the Hon. Odo Vivian's handwriting.

29

Eppynt Mountains Premium Show, Cwmowen Inn, 5 May 1917. Presiding were Mr F. Carter (Board of Agriculture), Mr Coltman Rogers (judge), Mr J. F. Rees MRCVS, Mr J. R. Bache (WCPS secretary), and Mr J. L. Davies (local secretary).

a half by one mile). The four stallions were all of showring standard, every one being either a son or grandson of the redoubtable Dyoll Starlight.

At Penybont, apart from two stallions lent to the society, their stallions and mares turned out to be of a very low standard. Nevertheless they could end up as useful animals in a few generations of careful breeding. The Gwynfe ponies were regarded as a most promising lot, the hills (of ten miles length and seven miles width) being composed of that limestone formation regarded as being the best geological prescription for the conformation and development of equines. The four stallions, although different in type, were all praiseworthy. Proceedings did not finish with judging the stallions; speeches had to be delivered in English and Welsh and a poem was composed in honour of the occasion, delivered by a local celebrity from a platform of beer cases at the back of a more substantially built pigsty!

Unfortunately the judges had to remark on the impoverished and bare-boned condition of animals presented at several centres. Many were in 'ribs of wreck' condition, never having been the recipient of so much as a kindly thought let alone a chance wisp of hay. It was in 1916 that graduated premium awards were started, of £7, £5 and £3 instead of the previous £5 'all round'. The intention was that owners would be encouraged to produce their animals in better condition to aim at £7.

Some of the top lowland breeders who were not eligible for the premium scheme co-operated by lending valuable and fashionably bred stallions to premium societies. Mrs Greene of Grove Stud in 1916 lent two to Eppynt and one each to Penybont and Church Stretton. The cost of presentation and travelling from the Grove absorbed the greater part (if not all) of the premium award, and Mrs Greene was warmly thanked for sending some of her best ponies to a rather problematical destiny in strange lands.

The Church Stretton inspection on 11 April 1918 was a day full of surprises. Three of the stallions entered in the programme failed to put in an appearance; two of them, Stretton Klondyke and Stretton Sweep, had avoided the many attempts to catch them on the hills! The other absentee, Gwyndy Prizeman, was described as 'about done in'. The ravages of time and wear and tear of a long life upon the hilltops had obviously brought his career to an end. The judges awarded a premium to Mr Beddoe's pony by the brilliant Bleddfa Shooting Star, but the commoners refused to have him. The judges then awarded a premium to Mr Fred Hill's piebald stallion, Ap Starlight by Dyoll Starlight. The commoners were prepared to accept this stallion readily, but it turned out that the owner had no intention of allowing his 'pride and joy' loose on any hills. He had only brought him there since he liked showing and all other 'shows' had been cancelled during the war years!

An interesting fact is that Mr J. F. Rees, MRCVS, who accompanied the premium judges and Board of Agriculture representatives for almost twenty years, subjected each stallion to a minute and very exhaustive examination, and despite poor condition and their wild lives on high ground, never once did he find a stallion who had to be rejected on veterinary grounds. Defective genital organs, which one regularly finds amongst current native ponies and Cobs, are therefore of comparatively recent origin.

One sad incident to record was the sudden lack of enthusiasm that had appeared in the Carmarthenshire Black Mountain Society by 1918. The poets had disappeared and the complete local picture consisted of three young colts and one solitary spectator.

Messrs J. R. Bache and H. Meyrick Jones (Mathrafal) were the judges in 1919. Stretton Klondyke at Longmynd allowed himself to be caught and was awarded a premium. Stretton Sweep and Gwyndy Prizeman were not heard of again.

The first time on record (also 1919) that one stallion who had proved his worth for one society was bought by another was when Captain Christy of Llyswen (Christy's hats) purchased Ragleth Rocket from Mrs Gibbon of Little Stretton for the use of the Eppynt commoners. One stallion on Eppynt was described as 'too long in his couplings and animals too long in their barrels are inclined to be of the soft sort'.

The 1920 judges at Eppynt (Cwmowen) regretted that the two best stallions of the previous year had been sold to go 'down the pits'. Enthusiasm had returned to Gwynfe; Mr Herbert was back from the war and he soon drummed up enthusiasm to regain their old high standards. The top stallions received £10, the middle stallions £7 and the last stallions £5. There was good competition at most centres, with seven premiums awarded on Eppynt, eight at Church Stretton, four at Gwynfe (Black Mountains), three at Fairwood and one at Cefn Bryn.

As a result of the Horse Breeding Act of 1918 every stallion had to be licensed annually by veterinary inspection before it could receive a premium.

In the 1920s the premium scheme flourished, but the reduction of available funding from the Chancellor of the Exchequer, known as the 'Geddes axe' (which also curtailed many other activities in Wales such as education), fell in 1922 and the Board of Agriculture was no longer in a financial position to continue the grant. However, the War Office realised the necessity of horses and ponies in any war effort, and offered to continue the grant temporarily.

Typical of the success of the scheme was the 1928 judging, when eight stallions were awarded premiums at Radnorshire Beacon Hill (out of 20 stallions presented); two stallions at Rhos Fallog Hill; five stallions at the Great Forest of Brecon (Van), where the well-known Hardwick Conqueror was third; three stallions at Mynydd Bwlch-y-Groes, with Ness King and Caer Beris Diamond, two stallions who had won at major shows, standing first and second; four stallions at Fairwood (Mathrafal Rascal was fourth); three at Cefn Bryn; the two good stallions Faraam Cocoa Nibs and Crossways Shon o'r Lleyn were awarded premiums at Llanrhidian; nine stallions out of 14 were awarded premiums at Church Stretton, with Bowdler Baron II, sire of the elegant Coed Coch Seirian, standing seventh; 13

out of 18 at Eppynt, including Gwibedog Ballet Dancer (fifth) and Caer Beris Donovan (eighth); four out of seven Black Mountains (Eastern, at Talgarth); and six out of nine at Black Mountains (Carmarthenshire, at Gwynfe).

Britain experienced a period of unparalleled depression during the early 1930s. This was reflected within the Welsh Pony and Cob Society by the publication of its stud books in stencilled form rather than its customary printed green volumes. In 1932, the Treasury withdrew the grant which it had previously made to the War Office to subsidise stallions, so in 1932 and 1933 no premiums were offered to Welsh Mountain pony stallions to run loose on the Commons, or to Welsh Cob stallions to be travelled around Wales. During 1932 and 1933 the majority of the Hill Pony Improvement Societies either ceased their activities altogether or curtailed them drastically. The War Office officials were sympathetic towards horse and pony breeding but had to cut down national expenditure to the absolute minimum. By 1934 the situation had improved marginally, and the Treasury voted the War Office a reduced sum (the grant to Thoroughbred stallions of £18,000 per annum in 1932 was reduced to £4,000 in 1934). This was boosted by an additional grant from the Racecourse Betting Control Board which has thankfully continued to the present day.

The scheme funded jointly by the War Office and the Racecourse Betting Control Board (now the Horserace Betting Levy Board) continued successfully until the outbreak of war. A typical premium stallion competition is shown below at Eppynt (2 May 1938), amidst the bleak vegetation of Welsh hill land.

Eppynt premium stallions, 1938: the winner was Duhonw Emperor (*right*), owned by Mrs L. M. Evans; second and third, both owned by Mr John Griffiths, were Revel Bluestone (*centre*) and Revelation (*nearest camera, held by Mr Emrys Griffiths*).

Black Mountains (Eastern section) premium stallions being judged in 1956 at the Revel.
(*Photo: Beacon Studios, Brecon*)

During the war years the premiums were sponsored by the Racecourse Betting Control Board alone, and premiums were awarded every year at Church Stretton, Eppynt and the Black Mountains. Such influential stallions as Bowdler Blue Boy, Caer Beris Imaway, Mathrafal Windfall, Square Flashlight, Revel Brightlight, Revel Chief, Duhonw Emperor, Criban Monty, Criban Winston, Llwyn Tom Tit, Mathrafal Tuppence, Revel Wampus, Criban Grey Grit and Revel Atom Swell took part. Premiums for Fairwood (Gower), Mynydd Illtyd, Vaynor and Pontsarn and Aber Hills (Bangor) were suspended for the war years, but then resurrected with such good stallions as Ness King, Ness Commander, Craven Tit Light (later exported to Australia), Revel Springlight (sire of Royal Welsh champion Revel Caress), Coed Coch Samswn and Criban Flag Day.

Judging premium stallions in the 1950s took the best part of a week. The two judges started in North Wales at the Aber Hills, Bangor (one premium) and Denbigh Moors (two premiums), followed by Church Stretton (two premiums), then coming south to Mid-Wales: Elan Valley (three premiums), Beggins Hill (Radnorshire, one premium), Llanafan (four), Eppynt (twelve), Black Mountains

34

(East, eight), Black Mountains (Brynamman, one), Llandefalle (two), Aberyscir (one), Brecon Beacons (two); and finally to South Wales: Gower (two), Penderyn (four), Dowlais and Twynrodyn (five), Manmoel (one) and Ebbw Vale (two). The photograph opposite shows the 1956 judging of the Black Mountains (Eastern Section) premium stallions at the Revel Farm, Talgarth, where the result was as follows: 1st – Owain Glyndwr (exported to USA), 2nd – Gaerstone Guardsman, 3rd – Bowdler Brewer (champion of the 1961 Royal Welsh Show), 4th – Coed Coch Watcyn, 5th – Gaerstone Brightlight, 6th – Kilhendre Celtic Silver Birch, 7th – Revel Springlight and 8th – Criban Winston. Other champion stallions to be awarded premiums during 1956 were Vardra Sunstar (Dowlais) (sire of Royal Welsh champion Revel Choice), Criban Bantam (Vaynor), Eryri Gwyndaf and Ceulan Revelry (Gower), Pendock Zenith (Beggins Hill), Glascoed Mervyn (Elan) and Criban Atom (Eppynt).

To save the judges having to travel around Wales an experiment was tried out in 1960 to combine some of the premium stallion judging with the Glanusk One-day Horse Trials held at Glanusk Park, Crickhowell. The premium classes were judged in conjunction with some open classes for stallions, which produced such famous names as Coed Coch Madog, Criban Bantam, Coed Coch Socyn, Meredith of Maen Gwynedd (sired by premium stallion Owain Glyndwr), Pendock Zenith (a former premium stallion and sired by premium winner Vardra Sunstar), Coed Coch Siglen Las and Coed Coch Salsbri. The experiment proved to be such a success that the following year it was extended to include all the premium classes for Wales. This show continued in the picturesque setting of Glanusk Park until 1969, when the site was no longer able to contain the greatly expanded and successful show, so it was moved to the Royal Welsh Showground. There it has gone from strength to strength, with 480 entries competing at the 1990 show in the 24 classes for sections A, B, C and D stallions and youngstock, and 38 stallions competing for premiums to spend the summer running out in 16 Pony Improvement Society areas.

The premium stallions were (and still are) turned out on the hills and Commons around the end of May, one stallion to about every 15 to 20 mares. The stallion and his harem would be turned out one day and given time to settle and go far enough away, and then if other stallions with bands of mares were to be turned out on the same hill, this procedure was repeated with each one. Only very rarely would a mare desert one stallion and go to join another stallion's band should the two bands come into contact during the summer. This is how the owners knew the sires of their foals for registration purposes; usually the owner would have made frequent

Premium stallions at Eppynt, 1954: (*right to left*) Mr T. Wilson's Cui Hailstone and Messrs W. Davies and Son's Ceulan Revolt (*equal first*); Mr W. M. Price's Bolgoed Pippin, Mr T. J. G. Price's Dyrin Athlete and Mr J. B. Jones's Criban Trilby (equal third). The judges at the left are Mr Campbell Moodie (Canada House), Mr R. Douglas Evans, and Mr I. Osborne Jones.

visits to the bands of stallions with their mares anyway so knew the sires of the foals. Rarely a mare which had been in the company of one stallion but turned out with a different one might revert to the previous stallion if they had a chance meeting later on. But in most cases, especially with stallions who had served their time on the hills, the stallions would savagely drive off any marauding stallions with their mares that they might encounter as they changed their grazing areas. Some stallions which had enjoyed a pampered upbringing on lowland studs were not so successful in guarding their bands, and for others the climate would be too harsh, but the majority, even if lowland bred, enjoyed their freedom and prospered amidst the haunts of their fore-fathers.

The lasting influence of premium stallions over 80 years is well described by studying Maescwm Trumpeter (light cream chestnut, eel stripe and zebra markings, 1980), champion premium stallion in 1990. He is out of Maescwm Martini (dun 1967) who was by Crwydryn Brodrick (premium); granddam Cwmowen May Bee (dun, eel stripe, 1953) by Cwm Cream Dandy (premium); great granddam Cwmowen Lucy (chestnut 1945) by Criban Monty (premium); great great granddam Cwmowen Lady (dun, eel stripe, 1931) by Forest Blue Banner (premium); great great great granddam Cwmowen Young Cream Nellie (dun, 1911), one of the original mares running out on Eppynt at the time of the premium judging at Cwmowen on 5 May 1917.

Maescwm Trumpeter, champion premium stallion 1990, shows the lasting influence of premium stallions. (*Photo: Wynne Davies*)

# 4 Export and sales

Reference was made at the 1909 Annual General Meeting of the Welsh Pony and Cob Society to the exciting development which had occurred that year: the export of six Welsh Mountain pony stallions and 27 mares from the 'Forest' Stud of Mr W. S. Miller (including some daughters of Klondyke) to the USA and Canada. Exports kept up in 1910, with one stallion and nine Forest mares going to Canada, and five Grove mares going to the USA. Interest received a great boost in 1911 when a Cob stallion and 12 mountain pony mares were sold to the Mount Horeb Stud in Australia, along with six mares and the stallions Cream of Eppynt, Merry Boy and Greylight to Mr Anthony Hordern CBE of the Milton Stud. Greylight (foaled in 1900) was described as 'the World's most perfect pony and the only pony ever to have a Royal Command to appear before Queen Alexandra'. He was sold for £1,000 (equivalent to about 50 times this figure today). This trade provided extra income to South Wales farmers who were going through lean times.

Greylight, one of the most beautiful of stallions.

Additional encouragement was provided by the American Department of Agriculture by exempting from import duty (after 1 January 1911) animals which were registered within the Welsh Pony and Cob Society Stud Book. In 1912, 116 Mountain ponies went to the USA. There were 13 stallions, six of which came from Mrs H. D. Greene of the Grove Stud; three from Mr J. Marshall Dugdale (Llwyn); one from Mr Evan Jones (Towyvale); one from Mr W. S. Miller (Forest); and two from Mr W. J. Roberts (Longmynd). The 103 mares consisted of 31 from Llwyn, 24 from Grove, 19 from Forest, 13 from Longmynd, six from Messrs Hamar and Sons (Bicton), four from Mr W. Arthur Pughe (Gwyndy), four from Mr B. D. Benbow (Stretton) and two from Mr W. J. Cooke (Coppice).

Mr W. S. Miller of the Forest Stud, Forest Lodge, Brecon would have 200 or more ponies roaming on the Brecon Beacons around this time. American Mrs Olive Tilford Dargan, who in 1913 printed privately a 52-page book for Mr Charles A. Stone (which prompted Mr Stone to import 25 Mountain ponies!), included a photograph of the 'Forest' ponies taken 'one Sunday morning when I sallied out unmoved by the church-bells, which chime so indefatigably in Welshland, and climbed the highest, craggiest hill in sight'.

Many Breconshire farmers had kept herds of Mountain ponies for many generations, as is seen from the '12 Mountain Ponies of different ages, size, and colour of the real Brooks Lwener breed' advertised for sale by auction at Penllwynyrhendy Farm, Sennybridge, in 1861.

An innovation instigated by Mr Dugdale's Llwyn Stud is reported in the 1905 *Livestock Journal*, and this was to sell consignments of their ponies at Tattersall's Sales in London. The prices of 31 guineas and 40 guineas obtained for 12-hand Welsh Mountain ponies in 1905 are equivalent to £1,500 to £2,000 today.

The most notable innovation as regards the sale of ponies from this stud was their first annual sale at Tattersall's in June. Perhaps, as it was their first sale, they were wise in only sending four ponies. The prices realised were quite satisfactory, two mares, 12 hands, fetching 40 gs. and 31 gs. In future, I understand that they intend sending up eight or ten really good, reliable ponies.

It seems to me that it would be a move in the right direction if a combination of breeders were formed and some concerted action taken to secure a suitable day for holding a special sale of ponies of the stamp sent up by Mr Dugdale last year. Everybody is asking for reliable ponies for ladies and children, and if only it had been known where they are to be found, customers would certainly not be wanting.

A more ambitious venture was operated by Mr Evan Jones of Manoravon when he shipped consignments of animals to Australia and held auctions in Sydney.

Minutes of the 1920 WPCS AGM record: 'Efforts were made to resuscitate the WPCS Annual Sales which were held pre-war. A Sale was held at Lampeter on 5 May 1920 but it was not a success.' Sales organised by the WPCS and held in Craven Arms were more successful, starting with the 6 September 1922 sale where 200 ponies were offered, including 39 from Grove Stud and 29 from Kilhendre Celtic. At this sale, eight classes were held with prize money of £2 and £1 for animals which were offered for sale, the judges being Mr Ffitch Mason of Gower, Mr T. B. Lewis (Llanwrtyd Wells) and Mr W. S. Miller (Forest Lodge, Brecon). Well-known ponies offered for sale here included Grove Elfin, Bwlch Quicksilver, Lochtyn Tosca, Grove Peep O'Day, Forest Mountain Model and Mathrafal Wampus.

Annual sales were held by auctioneers Frank Lloyd and Sons of Wrexham, starting with a very successful sale held on 27 September 1952 with 80 ponies offered. Top prices were reached of 76 guineas for Ceulan Stud's Ceulan Cora to the Duchess of Rutland, and 74 guineas for Gredington Stud's Bowdler Blue Berry, sold to the USA.

Jones Brothers, Auctioneers of Builth Wells, conducted outdoor sales on the Eppynt Mountains at Llanafan-fawr and Cwmowen Inn. In the heyday of pony sales these two sales were very well attended and very good prices were obtained for foals straight off the hills. These sales still continue and serve a convenient outlet for local breeders.

Annual sales were also held for many years at the Foxhunter Stud at Abergavenny, Gurnos Stud in Merthyr Tydfil and the Gredington Sales at Bangor-on-Dee. The first Fayre Oaks Sale took place on 9 October 1954 at the Fayre Oaks Stud Farm, Kings Acre Road, Hereford, with auctioneers Jackson and McCartney of Craven Arms. There were 65 ponies sold from the Fayre Stud, along with seven from Mrs Cuff, who then lived at Bucknell, Shropshire, and seven from Cusop Stud. Top-priced Mountain pony stallion was Revel Blue Banner (40 guineas), and the top-priced mare at the same figure was Fayre Black Dawn, who went to start the Penllyn Stud at Cowbridge. A famous old mare, Craven Fairylight, who was the foundation mare of the Trefesgob Mountain ponies, sold for 26 guineas, and a

Downland yearling colt out of Craven Sprightly Twilight (granddam of Downland Chevalier) sold for 15 guineas.

The following year the auctioneers were Russell, Baldwin and Bright of Hereford. This occasion was the first introduction of these auctioneers (now the official auctioneers for the WPCS) to Welsh ponies and Cobs. The sale took place on the same site on 1 October 1955, with 23 ponies from Dyrin, 22 from Fayre, 16 from Coed Coch, 10 from the Revel, eight from Criban, eight from Cusop, four from Maen Gwynedd, two from Ceulan (who have offered ponies on every Fayre Oaks Sale since 1955), two from Pendock, two from Whitepool and one from Bwlch. Top price of 90 guineas was paid by Mrs Mountain of the Twyford Stud for Sundana of Maen Gwynedd, a two-year-old daughter of Clan Dana. Top-priced male at 48 guineas was Royal Reveller (bred at Ceulan), bought by Captain Homfray. Reveller was one of the very few stallions ever to have been able to beat the great Coed Coch Madog in the showring.

Prices remained about the same at the 1956 sale, where 33 vendors sold 169 ponies, and 15 colt and filly foals sold for between 13 and 44 guineas. By 1957 interest in Welsh Mountain ponies had reached the USA and some Americans attended the sale. Mr Vern Rider of Newmarket, Virginia, asked me to buy 30 for him, which obviously gave a wonderful boost to the sale. The filly foals Revel Sugar Bun and Vaynor Jennifer went to the USA (along with another 20) at 250 and 225 guineas respectively. With Mr Rider being under-bidder on many other lots, Mr Hayes of Sutton Coldfield had to pay 230 guineas for Revel Seafoam, and Lord Kenyon 180 guineas for Revel Belinda.

The 1958 sale, with 240 entries, was the last to be held at the Fayre Oaks Stud. The stabling and facilities there were unable to cope with such increased numbers, so the sale was moved to Hereford Market. By 1960 entries had increased to 492 and the sale was extended to Friday and Saturday. In 1962, a separate 'Fayre Stud' sale of 88 ponies was held on the Friday at the stud, which by then had moved to Dorstone, with a Saturday sale of 325 entries at Hereford. From 1963 to 1970, over 30 per cent of all animals sold went to the continent, with 1,600 ponies exported in 1967. This attracted record entries of 841 in 1969 and 842 in 1970, so the sale was held on Saturday, Monday and Tuesday. Entries started to decrease by 1975 and the sale reverted to Friday and Saturday.

Average prices have unfortunately not kept pace with the retail price index. The average figure of £144 in 1965 increased to a high of £230 in 1973, went down to £141 in 1983 and up to £285 in 1988.

Revel Springbok, a four-year-old palomino son of the 1957 Royal Welsh champion Revel Springsong, was the first animal to fetch 1,000 guineas on the Fayre Oaks Sale, in 1967. This was followed by good prices for the mare Coed Coch Perot (950 guineas) and the stallion Twyford Matador (925 guineas) in 1968. Other highlights were Aston Garway (900 guineas, 1971), Carnalw Hyderus (880 guineas, 1975), Rowfant Seal (1,400 guineas, 1976), Weston Anniversary (1,900 guineas, 1980), Synod Scamp (1,000 guineas, 1979), Derwen Eclipse (filly foal, 900 guineas, 1980), Weston Pearly Necklace (1,500 guineas, 1982), Coed Coch Bleddyn (2,500 guineas, 1985), Vimpenny Chamomile (1,500 guineas, 1986), Dryfe Sheer Heaven (yearling, 1,400 guineas, 1987), Moorcock Fairytale and Trisant Pansy (filly foals, 950 and 800 guineas, 1987), Synod Dicky Bow (colt foal, 750 guineas, 1987), Sunwillow Monte Rosa (2,400 guineas, 1988), Springbourne Halwyn (1,500 guineas, 1988), Foxhunter Parakeet (2,200 guineas, 1989), Fronbach Hello Dandy (colt foal, 1,400 guineas, 1989), Bengad Wallflower and Gwyn Rhosyn Emmerline (two mares at 1,400 guineas, 1990), and Synod Jonquil (filly foal, 900 guineas, 1990).

Fron Bach Hello Dandy (Synod Hello x Fron Bach Carys) who held the record (1,400 guineas in 1989) for a foal sold on the Fayre Oaks sale until overtaken by the filly foal Fron Bach Dyma Hi in 1991 (1,500 guineas). (*Photo: Wynne Davies*)

Both Section A foal and adult record prices were exceeded at the 1991 Fayre Oaks Sale when Terry and Lyndon Foley of the Bronycoed Stud, Merthyr Tydfil, paid 3,600 guineas for the Hon. Mrs Monck's mare Lippens Dolly, and the foal record figure of 1,400 guineas for Fronbach Hello Dandy was broken when Fron Bach Dyma Hi sold for 1,500 guineas to Holland.

## The Welsh Mountain pony abroad

The increasing numbers of exports have lead to the establishment of studs and societies in a number of countries around the world, as detailed below.

Exports from all sections of the Welsh Stud Book to selected countries, 1957–1991

|  | 1957 | 1962 | 1967 | 1972 | 1977 | 1982 | 1987 | 1988 | 1989 | 1990 | 1991 |
|---|---|---|---|---|---|---|---|---|---|---|---|
| Australia | – | 3 | 1 | 4 | 50 | 4 | – | 11 | 5 | 4 | 9 |
| Belgium | 1 | – | 37 | – | – | – | 4 | – | 2 | 11 | 21 |
| Canada | 73 | – | – | – | – | – | 3 | 3 | 10 | – | 12 |
| Denmark | – | 15 | 43 | 116 | 4 | 3 | 16 | 11 | 7 | 21 | 19 |
| France | – | – | 36 | – | – | – | 7 | 3 | 10 | 12 | 14 |
| Germany | 1 | – | 33 | 257 | 79 | 24 | 27 | 32 | 72 | 70 | 65 |
| Holland | – | 33 | 573 | 1,403 | 73 | 33 | 33 | 34 | 30 | 21 | 56 |
| Sweden | 2 | 9 | 10 | 18 | – | 3 | 6 | 14 | 43 | 14 | 26 |
| USA | 472 | 18 | – | 1 | 1 | 18 | 15 | 10 | 8 | 5 | 6 |
| Total exports | 550 | 93 | 741 | 1,933 | 231 | 130 | 134 | 127 | 207 | 194 | 270 |
| Total UK registrations | 1,720 | 2,871 | 5,337 | 6,166 | 3,364 | 4,926 | 4,547 | 5,005 | 5,323 | 5,769 | 5,371 |
| Total UK membership | 560 | 1,850 | 3,593 | 5,575 | 6,400 | 6,800 | 6,350 | 6,550 | 6,449 | 6,836 | 6,834 |

## *Australia*

There are 1,100 members in the Welsh Pony and Cob Society of Australia and about 600–700 Welsh Mountain ponies are registered annually. Greatest emphasis is placed on in-hand showing, where the standard is exceptionally high, due to the import of some of the best animals from the UK as far back as 1910. In more recent times imports include the Royal Welsh Show champions Coed Coch Norman, Brierwood Rosebud, Valleylake Breeze, Rowfant Prima Ballerina, and the pony who reached the highest-ever price at a UK auction (21,000 guineas), Coed Coch Bari.

## Belgium

There are about 190 members in the Belgisch WP Stamboek, registering some 30 Mountain ponies annually. Pony Clubs are popular in Belgium and the ponies are regularly ridden by children.

## Canada

The Canadian WPC Society has over 300 members, registering about 120 Mountain ponies annually and incorporating some large studs of over 100 animals. The society was formed in 1894 with the largest boost to numbers being around 1955–60 when about 100 were imported annually.

## Denmark

The Danish WPC Avlen consists of 220 members registering about 150 Mountain ponies annually. The ponies are often driven in single or pair harness and teams of four, and are ridden, the preponderance of forest roads providing safe conditions for these activities.

## France

The emphasis in France is on the larger Section B ponies and Cobs. However, there are Mountain pony enthusiasts among the 50 or so members.

## Germany

There are 450 members in the Interessenge-meinschaft. Section B ponies and Cobs are in the majority, but there are some Mountain pony studs with very creditable animals, and driving them is becoming popular.

## Holland

There are two societies involved with the registrations of Mountain ponies in Holland, Het Nederlands WP Stamboek and the WPC Vereniging. They contain about 3,000 members, registering about 1,000 ponies annually. Stallions are given a strict inspection (involving riding and driving) every February. Driving is immensely popular, with driving classes to a show waggon often containing over 30

Welsh Mountain ponies in Holland: chariot racing. (*Photo: Ellen van Leeuwen*)

Welsh Mountain ponies in Holland: team of eight driven by Weremeus Buning. (*Photo: Wynne Davies*)

exhibits. Pair driving is also practised, along with teams of four (often to a 'Roman' chariot in 'Ben Hur' fashion) and spans of eight.

## Israel

About 20 Israelis keep Welsh Mountain ponies who thrive well in the hot climate and are largely looked after by children living in a kibbutz.

## New Zealand

Almost 300 members exist in the WPCS of New Zealand, registering annually about 80 Welsh Mountain ponies. Some very famous stallions were imported from the UK during 1970–80 to set a very high standard, e.g. Treharne Tomboy and Rondeels Pengwyn.

## South Africa

Despite the large distances involved, Welsh Mountain ponies turn up in numbers of 200 to 300 to compete at their annual National Show. Some very creditable animals were imported from 1948 to 1985 to guarantee a high standard. A single exhibitor often takes 20 to 50 ponies to compete, starting in hand, then pair and tandem harness and teams of four. The competition with spans of eight pulling a heavy 'gambo' at full gallop is most spectacular.

Driving spans of eight in South Africa.

## Sweden

There are 400 members in the Svenska Welsh Pony Foreningen and some 150 Mountain ponies are registered annually. The ponies are ridden by children and, to a lesser extent, driven, often to a sleigh in winter.

## Switzerland

With a similar membership to that of Sweden, there is greater emphasis on Welsh Cob breeding. However, there are small numbers of Mountain ponies bred which are very popular with children.

## United States of America

The WPCS of America, which boasts almost 1,000 members, was started in 1906 when about 100 ponies were imported from the UK. Between 1920 and 1950 fewer than 20 ponies were imported annually, this figure increasing dramatically to some 500 a year between 1955 and 1960. Currently it has steadied to about 20 a year once more. There are some very large studs in the USA, concentrating on in-hand showing, though children's riding is recently creating considerable interest. Single harness driving has always been popular, and to this end the American exhibitors have developed a 'refined' type of high-stepping pony, very different from the 'native' type. These are in a minority though they have a dedicated following.

## Other countries

In the last decade, Welsh Mountain ponies have also been exported in limited numbers to Brazil, Czechoslovakia, Dubai, Finland, Italy, Malta, Oman and Portugal.

# 5 Influential studs

To pinpoint 10–15 studs which have had the greatest influence on the development of the Welsh Mountain pony would be an impossible task. Some studs, though having bred numerically small numbers (for example, Mathrafal Stud registered only 35 ponies in the 65 years from 1873 to 1938), bred some very influential animals; other studs kept much larger numbers (e.g. Weston Stud sold 286 ponies by auction in its 22 years' existence (1957–79), and Coed Coch had 244 ponies at the stud when the dispersal sale took place in 1978).

Within the limited space of the present book, priority has been given to studs which are no longer in existence, or which continue only with minimal numbers (e.g. Revel and Cui).

## Craven Stud

Mr Tom Jones Evans was born in 1876, the second of 13 children of Dafydd Evans, Llwyncadfor, Henllan, in South Cardiganshire. Dafydd Evans reigned supreme in Cambrian cobland as the moulder of the destinies of Welsh Cobs in early Victorian days, and was one of three persons on whom Honorary Membership of the Welsh Pony and Cob Society was conferred in 1905, along with Mr Hill of Church Stretton and Sir Richard Green-Price of Presteigne. He died in 1918 and the family presented the magnificent David Evans, Llwyncadfor Memorial Cup which is competed for annually at the United Counties Show for the best Welsh Mountain pony stallion. I am looking at the trophy as I write this chapter, having been fortunate enough to win it in 1990.

The eldest son, David (1874–1947), stayed on to farm at Llwyncadfor, and for the first years kept a few Cobs and ponies. He sold six at the 1923 WPCS Collective Sale at Craven Arms, where his brother Tom Jones Evans was by then living. Tom often stayed at my home at Talybont and I well remember in the 1940s listening spellbound as he would relate how, when the stud season at Llwyncadfor was over around 1910 to 1920, he would harness one of the stallions to a light gig and drive around Wales, as far as Anglesey, to collect the stud fees. The collecting from Llwyncadfor to Anglesey would take about three weeks.

There were several exhibits (and winners) from Llwyncadfor at the early Royal

Tom Jones Evans (1876–1950), a great showman and judge of all breeds of horses and ponies.

Welsh Shows from 1904, with prize money of £10:£5:£2. Some were quoted as being 'for sale' at prices between £40 and £100.

The Welsh Mountain pony stallion Bleddfa Shooting Star was leased from Sir Walter Gilbey to stand at stud at Llwyncadfor for two seasons, but he was not patronised as well as he should have been. Some of his offspring from this period were Blaentwrch Firefly and Menai Queen Bess (both foaled in 1914), and two mares bred by Evan Jones the blacksmith of Caerwedros, both foaled in 1915, who became foundation mares of Mr Lyell's Ness Stud in Cheshire: Ness Sunflower and Ness Thistle. In the same way that Tom Jones Evans selected these two mares for Mr Lyell, he had 'discovered' some of the most successful ponies for the Grove Stud of Mrs H. D. Greene, and when Dinchope Farm became vacant on the Grove estate in 1921, he was offered the tenancy. And so he moved some 120 miles from

Newcastle Emlyn in Cardiganshire to Craven Arms in Shropshire. Mr Evans married Edith in 1911 but she died in 1934 and there were no children. That year Gladys (Mrs Douglas Meredith) became housekeeper at Dinchope and Douglas Meredith took over the tenancy. Douglas kept the 'Craven' prefix going until his death in 1984, the prefix now being the property of his daughter-in-law.

When Tom Jones Evans moved to Dinchope the Grove Stud was in its hey-day, winning countless championships with Grove King Cole II, Grove Moonstone, Grove Lightheart, Grove Fairy Queen, and so on, and he would never compete against his landlord. Indeed Mrs Greene was fortunate in having him as adviser, and he would often show the ponies for her and there was no better showman in the country.

On Wednesday, 29 June 1927, Mrs Greene dispersed her Grove Stud by auction on the premises. Mr Evans purchased the fifteen-year-old chestnut Grove Sprite II (dam of Grove Sprightly) and became joint-owner of Sprightly (with Lady Wentworth) for 126 gns. After the sale of the Grove ponies, Mr Evans started to show his own Mountain ponies and won the championship of the 1928 Royal Welsh Show with the eye-catching chestnut stallion Craven Master Shot, sired by Craven Star Shot (son of the aforementioned Ness Sunflower). Both Master Shot and Star Shot were later exported to the USA.

Grove Sprightly appeared in the sole ownership of Tom Jones Evans at the 1930 Royal Welsh Show and immediately romped away with the championship, a feat which he repeated every year until 1936. In order to give other exhibitors a chance, Mr Evans was appointed to judge at the 1937 show, but Sprightly emerged again to take all before him in 1938 and 1939.

On Saturday, 3 October 1936, the Craven Stud of 25 Welsh ponies was dispersed (with the exception of Sprightly) by auction at the Craven Arms Horse Repository. Some very well-known ponies passed through the sale ring that day: Craven Sunset went to Mrs Pennell for 12 gns; Craven Sprightlight and Craven Comet (by Ceulan Comet) went to the Criban Stud, from where they were exported to the USA the following year; and Grove Will o' the Wisp, who stood second to Sprightly several times, fetched only 55 gns to go to Dinarth Hall, from where he was exported to Italy the following year.

Mr Evans had regretted holding the dispersal sale in 1936, and by 1939 had bought Ness Daffodil and Gatesheath Dainty (dam of Craven Daylight, a successful sire at the Fayre Stud, and Craven Dainty, dam of the Sunrising Stud's Penmor Lovely Lady, 1960 Royal Welsh Show winner). Craven Tosca was kept back on the

Grove Sprightly at 12 years, champion at Islington in 1930 on his first appearance in the sole ownership of Tom Jones Evans. Shown by Mr Evans's nephew Mr Dai Howe. (*Photo courtesy Mrs Ingersoll, USA*)

Grove Sprightly expertly shown by his owner Tom Jones Evans, as always 'on a long rein'.

1936 sale and was given to the Pendock Stud in 1947, for whom she produced Pendock Playboy, sire of the 1957 Royal Welsh Show champion Revel Springsong.

Grove Sprightly died in 1949 at thirty-one years old, and Tom Jones Evans would admit that out of all the dozens of Welsh ponies, Hackneys and Cobs that had brought him great fame all over the world, Sprightly was his special favourite. The last offspring to be sired by Sprightly was Craven Sprightly's Last, foaled in 1945. She proved a very good producer for Mr Meredith, with among others Craven Sprightly Light, an RASE winner for the Fayre Stud before going to Australia, and Dovey Dynamite who won three first prizes at the Royal Welsh.

I remember seeing Sprightly at Dinchope in 1946 on our way home from the Shropshire and West Midland Show, and he looked 'regal' despite his twenty-eight years. He was buried at Dinchope and a gravestone erected in his memory. The gravestone was rescued (and is now at Cascob Stud) when Dinchope and Grove were demolished to be built over.

The third of the Llwyncadfor children was J. Morgan Evans (1881–1959), who spent most of his life with the Milk Retailers Association in London for which service he was awarded the MBE. Morgan Evans was also a WPCS judge and judged at the 1947 Royal Welsh Show and at the 1956 Bath and West Show. Others of the children included Mrs Howe, mother of Dai Howe who was at Dinchope for many years and later stud groom at the Dalhabbock Stud of Miss M. D. Russell-Allen.

Tom Jones Evans served as member of Council of the Welsh Pony and Cob Society from 1921, was vice-president in 1921–2 and president in 1931–2. Until 1948, WPCS Council members were elected on a 'County' basis. In 1949 members of Council were elected by postal ballot of every member, and for the first result Tom Jones Evans topped the election with 85 votes. He judged the children's riding ponies at the 1947 Royal Welsh Show and won the Hackney championship of the same show with his Craven Spotlight. 'Craven' ponies and Cobs were well represented in other ownerships and accounted for many of the prizes. There was no Royal Welsh Show in 1948 due to the petrol crisis, but again in 1949 there were four 'Craven' mares in the Mountain pony broodmare class: Mrs Cuff's Craven Good Friday and Craven Bright Sprite, Whitehall Stud's Craven Lymm, and Criban Stud's Craven Moonlight. There were also two stallions on show: Whitehall Stud's Craven Titbit and Mr Edgar Herbert's Craven Daylight.

Mr Evans, although obviously in failing health, attended the 1950 Royal Welsh Show where again the influence of the Craven Stud was very much in evidence. He then judged at the National Hackney Show in Bognor Regis, but that was his last public appearance. When he died on 14 October 1950, the horse world lost a showman and judge of all breeds of horses and ponies *par excellence*.

## Manoravon Stud

Mr Evan Jones (born in 1851 in Cardiganshire) went to Manoravon, Llandeilo in 1871 to become estate manager for Mr David Pugh MP. He very soon established a noted herd of Shorthorn cattle and stud of Welsh ponies and Cobs. When Mr Pugh died in 1890, Evan Jones bought Manoravon with its substantial mansion house and 650 acres of parkland and riverside meadows in the picturesque valley of the Towy, to add to his own 280 acres at Werville Brook, Cross Inn, Llandysul and Lochtyn, Llangrannog (the latter now owned by the National Trust). No expense was spared in setting up the herd of cattle (some being bought for sums between £300 and £1,500, figures which can be multiplied by 50 to bring up to today's values)

Manoravon (now known as Crumlyn Manor), Llandeilo. The stable block is on the left at the back. (*Photo: Wynne Davies*)

or the stud of Welsh ponies and Cobs. Evan Jones was an agriculturalist many years ahead of his time; he gave a lecture on how to make silage almost 100 years ago, most Welsh farmers only catching up with him 50 years later. He was also the pioneer for holding annual sales of Shorthorn bulls in Australia, sales to which consignments of Welsh ponies and Cobs, Hackneys and Shires were added around 1910.

A newspaper report in the *South Wales News* of 18 July 1928 relates how Evan Jones tried to form a Welsh Pony and Cob Society in 1898 by convening a public meeting at the Cawdor Arms, Llandeilo, but only one person (Mr Davies of Beulah) turned up. Evan Jones called another meeting to which Mr Price of Nantyrharn and Mr W. S. Miller of Forest Lodge turned up, and it was as a result of this meeting that six breeders assembled at the 1900 Show in Cardiff, and ten interested persons met at Llandrindod Wells on 25 April 1901 and laid the foundations of the WPCS. Evan Jones was immediately elected a member of Council of the WPCS and was vice-president for the years 1908–9.

In Volume 1 of the WSB there are 15 mares registered from Manoravon. They were foaled between 1885 and 1896 and measured between 12 and 14 hands. Five of them were sired by the 15-hand Welsh Cob stallion, King Flyer, and most had produced foals by Towyvale Squire, who was not himself registered in the WSB. Amongst the mares was Myfanwy, foaled in 1893. She was bred by Mr H. Williams of Carngerwchfawr and measured 12 hands 3 in. She later achieved great fame as dam of the legendary Greylight (foaled in 1900), sired by Dyoll Starlight who resided at nearby Glanyrannell, Llanwrda.

The Towyvale prefix was adopted in 1902, but only a few of the Manoravon ponies and Cobs were registered under this or the Wervillebrook or Lochtyn prefixes. Some did not have a prefix at all and some were registered with the Manoravon prefix.

The annual Manoravon sale was an important date in the calendars of pony and Cob breeders. A variety of farm stock was included on the annual sale, for example, in the sale held on 15 October 1913, 50 Welsh ponies and Cobs, 30 cattle and 50 draft ewes were sold, the yearling colt out of Myfanwy (dam of Greylight) fetching only £7. The Manoravon sales were a truly social event. Newspaper reports the following day listed the people present including Sir Gilbert Greenall, Warrington; Mr Depeaux, Paris; Mr Houston, Glasgow; Mr Baxter, Essex; and Mr Harrison, Manchester.

Mr and Mrs Evan Jones had six children, three boys and three girls. The eldest was Bill Price Jones who took the ponies and the Shorthorn cattle to Australia. The other two sons were Hugh, who spent many years in the Army and then farmed in Northampton, and David, who worked as an engineer in Britain and the USA but returned to Llandeilo to retire. The daughters were Mrs Williams (still alive at 101 years old in 1991), Mrs Enoch and Mrs Morgan.

In 1909 Bill Price Jones took out to Australia the two stallions Cream of Eppynt (foaled in 1906) and Merry Boy (foaled in 1902), and six mares: Norma, daughter of Merry Boy; Towyvale Roanie, daughter of Cream of Eppynt and Lady Helgwm, both bred by Evan Jones; Gwyndy Flyaway; and Little Queen and Topsy (both foaled in 1908) from John Jones and Son of Dinarth Hall. Fortunately these bloodlines have been carefully preserved in Australia and formed the foundation of Lady Creswick's Nattai Stud to which Greylight was added in 1911.

Greylight driven at Manoravon by Bill Price Jones. (*Photo courtesy of Robin Morgan*)

57

In 1911 Bill Price Jones took Greylight out to Australia to sell. He was exhibited at the 1911 Royal Melbourne Show and the following report appeared in the *Australian Daily Press*:

In the show arena Greylight shows himself off to perfection and he moves with a grace and elegance which is most fascinating. Frequently he is observed standing on his hind legs in evident delight of his own beautiful conformation and symmetry while all eyes seem to be on him. Lovers of the horse regard him as being as near the model of perfection of any animal which has ever been born. One of the Sydney visitors to the show was Mr S. Hordern who has recently returned from a tour through England where he purchased a number of stud animals of various breeds and yesterday it was announced that he had secured Greylight. Messrs Campbell and Sons of Kirk's Bazaar who negotiated the sale on behalf of the Welsh Stud master refuse to divulge the price but we have it on good authority that the figure was £1,050. It is intended to place Greylight at Stud this season in Victoria and his services have already been in great request by breeders and regret is expressed that such a valuable sire should be lost to this State. Some time ago the Victorian Government appointed a Commission to advise on the best way to improve horse breeding for remounts and the Commission of experts eventually recommended that the Government should import a number of Welsh sires but, as usual, the matter ended with the recommendation. Mr Hordern's enterprising spirit will be warmly approved of in New South Wales. Greylight forms the frontispiece to the pictorial Show Supplement for *The Leader* this week where he is featured in characteristic style on his hind legs.

And so it was that Greylight, who had been the idol of the showrings of Britain, was to spend the rest of his life in the far-away Antipodes. His moment of crowning glory had been at the Agricultural Hall, where he had been greatly admired by the Queen and Princess Victoria:

Her Majesty leaned forward in evident admiration, and all the house applauded loudly as the first of the ponies reached the level of the royal box. The pony was Mr E. Jones's Greylight, an animal as near perfection as any pony ever bred. He is a pure white stallion, and though under twelve hands has the graces, the flowing tail and mane, and more than the paces of a charger. The pony has no rival in Europe, and it was remarkable that in the class in which he won the first four – one white, two greys, one black – were all by the same sire.

A profitable occupation of many Mid-Wales pony breeders in the 1920s was to 'discover' animals with winning potential, produce them to win and sell them at a handsome profit to some of the leading showing studs of the day, such as Mrs Greene's Grove Stud or Mr Lyell's Ness Stud. Tom Jones Evans had found Ness Thistle from Caerwedros for Mr Lyell, and Nantyrharn Starlight from Brecon and Grove Fairy from the Gower for Mrs Greene; similarly Evan Jones found Towy Lady Moonlight (later re-named Grove Star of Hope) and Towyvale Delight for Mrs Greene. Towyvale Delight was bred by Mr Miller of Forest Lodge in 1920, sired by Forest Chief out of Forest Brave Lula by Forest Bravo. She won first prize at the 1924 NPS Show and first and champion medal at the 1926 NPS Show, plus first prize at the Reading RASE Show. In the 1927 Grove Stud Dispersal Sale catalogue she is described: 'At Islington 1926 she was said to be the finest piece of horseflesh in the whole show.' Evan Jones had sold her to Mrs Greene for 80 guineas, and on the sale she and her super little filly by Bleddfa Shooting Star went to the Misses May and Summers for 56 guineas. Her new owners did not produce her very well and at the Royal Welsh Show later that year she stood fifth to Kittiwake shown by my father for Dinarth Hall.

Another 'Forest' mare to be purchased was Forest Tosca, foaled in 1909, sired by Forest Ranger out of Forest Roan Lark by Forest Flash. Forest Tosca was re-

Towyvale Delight (by Forest Chief out of Forest Brave Lula). 'The finest piece of horseflesh' at the Islington Show in 1926.

59

registered as Lochtyn Tosca by Evan Jones, using his Lochtyn, Llangrannog address. Lochtyn Tosca bred (in 1916 by Kismet) Lochtyn Tissie, dam of Craven Sunset, whose progeny included Craven Titbit. Lochtyn Tosca was also dam of Craven Tosca, dam of the famous Pendock Playboy. Ninety-five per cent of the current Ceulan ponies trace back to him. Another influential bloodline was Towy-vale Myfy, a little chestnut mare foaled in 1905. A well-known winner all over Britain, she was sired by Dyoll Starlight out of Myfanwy, and was therefore full sister to Greylight. Towyvale Myfy spent many years at Miss Beryl Chapman's Kilhendre Celtic Stud, producing amongst others Kilhendre Celtic Silversand, sire of many dozens of good ponies at the Revel.

Thus the bloodlines of ponies bred by Evan Jones at Lochtyn and Manoravon had enormous influence on the Welsh Mountain pony breed, both in Britain and overseas. His services as a judge were often called upon at major shows, his last big judging appointment being at the 1919 RASE Show. He was a JP for the county of Carmarthen and, prior to this, a JP for his native county of Cardigan.

Evan Jones (1851–1936). A man many years ahead of his time; he tried to form a Welsh Pony and Cob Society single-handedly in 1898.

The Manoravon estate was sold on Saturday 21 July 1928, when Evan Jones was 78 years old, and he died in January 1936 aged 86. The Manoravon farm continues as a well-known and progressive dairy farm. The Manoravon mansion was kept until Mrs Jones's death in 1945 and was re-named Crymlyn Manor. It is now owned by the Thomas family and many famous cattle have been bred there, as well as a few Welsh ponies.

Grandson Robin Morgan is the proud possessor of one of Greylight's shoes, some of the trophies won by him and many WPCS medals won by all the Manoravon ponies and Cobs. Here at Ceulan, we have the Evan Jones Memorial trophy won by Dinarth What Ho for the best Welsh Mountain pony at Llandeilo Show, won in three consecutive years, 1950–2.

## Mathrafal Stud

The Mathrafal Stud had its greatest influence on the Welsh Pony and Cob Society via the Cob section, and, although it is not generally appreciated, it also had a major effect on Section B, since after its inauguration in the 1930s, the 1940s 'saviour' of this section was Criban Victor (foaled in 1944), whose grandsire was Mathrafal Broadcast, a son of Mathrafal Eiddwen. However, the Mathrafal Stud had no small part to play in Welsh Mountain pony evolution during the first 40 years of the WPCS, and the foundations laid at Mathrafal have been instrumental in the development of the breed, especially in the 'premium stallion' areas.

The first Mathrafal pony to be registered in the WSB was Mathrafal Beauty, a bay mare with black points of unknown parentage foaled in 1873, and she was a consistent prizewinner at Ruabon, Corwen, Llangollen, Mold and Wrexham Shows between 1884 and 1891. Her owner was Mrs J. Maurice Jones of Mathrafal Farm, Meifod, Montgomery, whose family was farming Mathrafal at the time of Beauty's birth. By the time of the birth of Mathrafal Rascal and Mathrafal Havoc (1914 and 1915), the two stallions which contributed very largely to the successful launch of the Church Stretton premium stallion scheme, the breeders were Mrs Jones's sons, Hugh Meyrick (born 1885) and Herbert Wynn (born 1887). Mr Meyrick Jones was by then a member of the WPCS Council and also an inspection judge. Advantage was taken of the American export trade in the early years and Mathrafal Blue Lass (foaled in 1906) and Mathrafal Megan (foaled in 1910) were exported to Frederick Bonney of Boston in 1913. Tragedy struck the family and Herbert was killed in the war in 1918, but Mr Meyrick Jones's interest in ponies was enhanced by having five

Welsh-bred riding ponies ridden by the Meyrick Jones daughters. *Left to right:* Welsh x TB, two Welsh x Arab, pure Welsh, and unknown x Welsh.

daughters who became very competent riders. Often all five would compete at a show in the children's riding classes, very often ending up with many of the prizes!

The influence of Mathrafal Havoc has gone to many parts of the world through his very famous son Bowdler Brightlight, who ended his days at the Farnley Stud in the USA. The other major Mathrafal influx into the USA happened when in 1950 two sons of Mathrafal Tuppence, namely Bolgoed Mighty Atom (foaled in 1939) and Bolgoed What Ho (foaled in 1940), went to the USA and started the pony harness craze out there. These two stallions created such a stir on the American harness scene that their photographs are still used to depict the 'harness' Welsh in the publications of the WPCS of America.

Mathrafal Tuppence was very ill as a foal in 1932, and was nursed by the Meyrick Jones daughters, who were very concerned that he would not live. He was named when the father remarked, 'Don't worry, he is not worth tuppence!' Luckily Tuppence survived and started his career as a very noteworthy sire, first at Mathrafal where he was also patronised by outside breeders, siring for example Brierwood Misty in 1936. Then he was sold to Criban Stud, where perhaps his best-known progeny was Criban Leading Lady, foaled in 1939. Mathrafal Tuppence was exchanged for Coed Coch Glyndwr in 1939 and his progeny in North Wales included Coed Coch Marchog, Coed Coch Serbysg and Eryri Gwyndaf, the stud stallion at Ceulan in 1947. Then Tuppence spent his time on the Breconshire Black Mountains, receiving premiums in 1941, 1944, 1945 and 1946.

The last stallion to be bred at Mathrafal, duly named Mathrafal Finalist, was foaled in 1938. His sire was Mathrafal Vim, who was also sire of Tuppence. Finalist's influence on the breed was via his granddaughter, the 1972 Royal Welsh Show champion Dyfrdwy Midnight Moon, and her son Aston Superstar who was Royal Welsh overall champion in 1978 and 1979. Mathrafal farm was sold in 1938 and Mr Meyrick Jones took the few remaining ponies with him to a farm in Bicester, but with the War Agricultural Committees demanding more grassland to be ploughed the ponies were disposed of. Mr Jones would often write to my home during the war years and obviously missed his ponies and Cobs. The last time I saw him was when he judged at the Aberystwyth Show in 1946, but he was taken ill that day and never really recovered. He died in 1950. Having been devoted to the WPCS for half a century it was sad that, having become president-elect, he died before he could take over the presidency.

With some studs registering 30 or 40 ponies every year, yet producing nothing

Mr Llewellyn Richards and Mathrafal Tuppence in 1938.

much of note, the exceptional feature of the Mathrafal Stud is that only 26 stallions and 31 mares, covering all sections of the Welsh Stud Book, were bred in 70 years, and yet the influence of Mathrafal has permeated Welsh pony and Cob breeding in its best aspect throughout the world.

Mr and Mrs Meyrick Jones at Mathrafal.

# Dyoll Stud

The signal honour of owning the animal given the registration number 1 of the Welsh Stud Book fell upon Mr Howard Meuric Lloyd, Glanyrannell, Llanwrda, with his Mountain pony stallion, Billy Bala. Had Mr Lloyd used his 'Dyoll' prefix (Lloyd spelt backwards), then for alphabetical reasons Dyoll Billy Bala would be number 3 in the WSB just before the world-famous Dyoll Starlight. Bred by Mr Lloyd in 1894, and number 4 in Volume 1 of the WSB, Dyoll Starlight's pre-eminence in the Welsh Mountain pony breed remains undisputed to this day.

Mr Lloyd was born in the West Indies in 1853. He returned to his family's estate at Danyrallt and Cynghordy in 1865 to be educated, later gaining his MA degree at Oxford before being called to the Bar. The Lloyd family was one of the oldest families in Wales, claiming direct descent from a British king in the fourth century, and each generation had played its part in the history of South Wales. The Danyrallt house was built in the sixteenth century. Mr Meuric Lloyd lived nearby at Glanyrannell Park, an impressive house which is today a flourishing hotel and guest house and home of a stud of Welsh Cobs. Mr Lloyd married his cousin Aimee Peel of Danyrallt in 1890 and they had five children, their daughter Lorna (Mrs Raleigh Blandy) living at Dolaubran, Cynghordy in 1991.

One or two Welsh ponies had been kept at Glanyrannell since 1884, but it was in 1890 with the purchase of Moonlight (registered in 1902 as Dyoll Moonlight) that the foundations of the Dyoll Stud were really laid. Mr Lloyd described this transaction:

> I went to see Mr Davies, Aberllechfach. It was on the eve of the fair held annually at Llanddeusant, close to the Carmarthen Van, our biggest mountain. He had some ponies gathered ready for the Fair and I went to see them. On his way from his farm he rode Moonlight up to where the others were. He said she was for sale and priced her at £13. I chose 2 others, the three came to £33.15.0 but I got them for £33.1.0; Moonlight I made out had cost me £12.

Moonlight was bred by Mr Thomas, the Pentre, in 1886, and carried the P brand of the Pentre (where Criban Biddy Bronze, who was so influential on Section B, was bred in 1950 by Mr Thomas's grandson). Moonlight was thought to be descended from the Crawshay Bailey Arab, turned out on the adjoining Brecon Beacons around 1850, and possibly from the Williams Aberpergwm Arab, running out there around 1840. Certainly Moonlight was more 'Araby' in appearance and with a 'silky' mane and tail (and grey in colour) than the 'Cobby' black, brown and dark bay hill ponies on which the 'Forest' ponies were founded.

In addition to the two stallions Billy Bala and Dyoll Starlight, Mr Lloyd registered 17 Mountain pony mares in Volume 1 of the WSB, all measuring under 12 hands and foaled between 1886 (Moonlight) and 1899. These mares were purchased from as far afield as Shrewsbury, Llangollen, Dolwyddelan and Bala. Moonlight is recorded as having won a first prize at Llandovery Show in 1896 and a second prize in 1899 at the Crystal Palace, London. One mare bought from John Williams, Gwernhefin, Bala, was named Dyoll Bala Gal (foaled in 1896). She was a little brown mare sired by one of the stallions running out on Gwastadrhos Hill. Her claim to fame was producing a bevy of famous animals, all sired by Dyoll Starlight: Dyoll Ballistite in 1903 (name changed to Grove Ballistite by 1907); Dyoll Radium in 1905; Dyoll Rainbow in 1907 (name changed to Grove Rainbow by 1911); Longmynd Eclipse in 1909; and the mares Dyoll Breeze in 1904 and Dyoll Spark in 1906. The export of Longmynd Eclipse to the USA is recorded in the 1913 WSB as 'regrettable and a sad loss to pony breeding of the Church Stretton area'; no doubt Mr W. Roberts, the Church Stretton schoolmaster who sold him for a good price, thought otherwise! One roan mare (foaled in 1888) bought from Mrs Jane Evans, Danrallt, Llandovery was registered as Dyoll Belinda. She does not seem to have produced anything at Dyoll but prior to purchase had produced Merlyn Myddfai, a well-known winning stallion (first prize at RASE Manchester in 1897 and second at Crystal Palace in 1899), who unfortunately was never registered but sired some very noted stock such as Star before being exported to Australia.

The most expensive mare to be purchased was Dyoll Quicksilver; a little black mare, she cost £25 since she had won 17 prizes in the Bala and Corwen areas of North Wales. Dyoll Quicksilver produced 11 foals by Dyoll Starlight, including Dyoll King Cole (foaled in 1905 and black like his mother), who was renamed Grove King Cole and exported to the USA in 1912 where he became a very successful harness pony. Grove King Cole at Grove sired Grove King Cole II, who in turn sired Caer Beris King Cole.                               —

Apart from Dyoll mares, outside mares flocked from far and wide for the services of Dyoll Starlight. Included amongst the progeny were Bleddfa Shooting Star out of Alveston Belle; Greylight out of Myfanwy; Bwlch Quicksilver out of Lady Greylight; the 10 full brothers and sisters out of Star, and so on. By 1912 there were 65 of his progeny registered in the WSB: 27 stallions (19 greys, 1 roan, 5 bays and

2 blacks) and 38 mares (22 greys, 5 roans, 4 bays, 3 browns, 2 blacks and 2 chestnuts).

The progeny took the showrings by storm. At the 1912 RASE Show at Norwich, all five stallions were by him, as was the champion mare Lady Starlight. At the Welsh National Show the first three stallions and first two colts were his sons, with his chestnut daughter Towyvale Myfy (sister of Greylight) being champion mare. In very strong competition at Church Stretton in the stallion class, of 11 entries (7 of them greys) every one was either his son or grandson!

Dyoll Starlight and his two most famous sons, Bleddfa Shooting Star and Greylight, proved indefatigable in the first 10 years of this century. It was Evan Jones and his staff at Manoravon who trained Starlight, and would never compete with Greylight against his sire. By 1911 Greylight had been shipped off to sunny Australia, and it was thought that Starlight had been retired to continue his humdrum reproductive life in the homely fastnesses of the Carmarthenshire hills; therefore it was quite a shock to all concerned to find the old patriarchal sire Starlight enter the showring at the 1913 Spring Polo Pony Society (NPS) Show at Islington, let alone stand at the head of the class with Shooting Star second. Contentious flames were soon ablaze and journalists added fuel to the fire. The

Dyoll Starlight winning the Mountain or Moorland pony stallion class at the RASE show at Maidstone, 1899, as a five-year-old. (*Photo courtesy of Mrs Lynn Spears*)

*Livestock Journal* didactically disagreed with the judge's verdict while *The Field* assented to the judgment. A few months later at the RASE Show at Bristol the same two stallions were found in juxtaposition; this time the tables were turned but surprisingly the *Livestock Journal* did not sing a song of exultation.

In 1919 Mr Lloyd's health began to fail and Dyoll Starlight was sold to Lady Wentworth at 25 years of age, on the understanding that he would never be sold and that, when he died, his skeleton would be presented to the British Museum in Mr Lloyd's name. Mr Lloyd died in 1922 and when his daughter Mrs Blandy returned from India in 1929 she failed to get Lady Wentworth to agree to let her see Starlight. It later transpired (in a letter which Lady Wentworth wrote to the magazine *Riding* in 1943) that Dyoll Starlight was sold to Spain in 1925 for £800 (equivalent to £17,000 in 1990) when he was 31 years old, and he had died there in 1929. In the same article Lady Wentworth claimed that Glasallt was not the sire of Dyoll Starlight since Glasallt had been gelded in 1893, and that Starlight's sire was Apricot, of Arab descent. It was pointed out to Lady Wentworth that Apricot had died 60 years before Starlight was born and that, anyway, Apricot lived on the Corwen hills 100 miles away. Lady Wentworth then suggested in her book *The World's Best Horse* that Dyoll Starlight was sired by a passing Arabian stallion. An emergency Council Meeting of the WPCS was called on 23 February 1944 to investigate the pedigree of Dyoll Starlight and Lady Wentworth's allegations, but on examining the detailed writings of Mr Meuric Lloyd it was decided without any doubt that the pedigree of Dyoll Starlight as recorded in the WSB was correct.

Mr Meuric Lloyd was a founder member of Council of the WPCS, representing Carmarthenshire, and vice-president for 1904–5. Mrs Blandy joined in 1923, and her services as judge were very much in demand. She was president for 1951–2 and elected an honorary life vice-president.

Between 1930 and 1965 Mrs Blandy bred several Welsh Cobs. One Mountain pony strain originating from Dyoll Moonstone (bred at Caer Beris in 1931) had to return to Foundation stock (Dyoll Tassel, foaled in 1940) by using an unregistered sire, Dyoll Tangle, and then up-graded via Dyoll Tinsel FS1 (foaled in 1954), Dyoll Timbrell FS2 (foaled in 1964) to Dyoll Thimble, fully registered, foaled in 1976. In 1991 there were four mares, including Thimble, at the Dyoll Stud. A Section B stallion used extensively at Janet Morgan's Cloigen Stud is Dyoll Thane. Son of Thimble and foaled in 1980, he is siring foals at Cloigen Stud exactly 100 years after the purchase of Dyoll Moonlight to start the Dyoll Stud.

The contents of Mrs Blandy's Dolaubran house were sold at Llandeilo Auction

Mr Meuric Lloyd (1853–1922), breeder of Dyoll Starlight in 1894, whose pre-eminence in the Welsh Mountain pony breed remains undisputed to this day.

Rooms on 18 September 1991. It is hoped that the stud records are in safe keeping but at the time of writing their whereabouts is not known.

## Cnewr Stud

Owner of the second-highest number of registered ponies in Volume 1 of the WSB in 1902, with 4 stallions and 21 mares (as compared with Mr W. S. Miller's 4 stallions and 46 mares at the Forest Stud), was Robert McTurk (Junior) of Cnewr, Sennybridge, Brecon. The Cnewr Estate was, up until 1819, part of the Great Forest of Brecknock, a royal hunting forest. In 1819 the Crown enclosed almost half the land and sold it (with the commoners who had historically paid to graze their stock on it losing out) to a merchant, John Cristie, who built a tramroad which contributed to his bankruptcy. The land was then sold to John Claypon, who extended the tramroad into the Swansea Valley.

In 1856 John McTurk from Kircudbright in Scotland rented Cnewr for his two sons Robert (senior) and Thomas, and when Robert married in 1869, Thomas returned to farm with his father in Kircudbright and Galloway. The two brothers were aged 22 and 18 when they started farming Cnewr, and portraits of them hang on either side of the fireplace in the dining room at Cnewr. By 1870 the McTurks were farming about 12,000 acres in Breconshire, although it was not until 1889 that they had the opportunity to purchase the main block of Cnewr. The labour force reached about 20 and the sheep flocks over 7,500 of Cheviot and Scottish black-faced sheep, which were walked from Crewe railway station (about 100 miles) on their way from Scotland to Cnewr.

The four stallions registered by Robert McTurk in Volume 1 were Clinker (foaled in 1892), Pompey (foaled in 1891), Pompey II (foaled in 1899) and Linesman (foaled in 1895). All four stallions were browns or dark bays. There was more variety in colour amongst the 21 mares: 14 were browns, blacks or dark bays, but there were two 'mousey duns', two creams, two greys and one whose name and colour was 'Khaki'!

By 1905 the 'Cnewr' prefix had been recorded with the WPCS and registrations in Volume 3 include the stallions Cnewr Goldfinder and Cnewr Black Jack, and the mares Cnewr Cherry, Cnewr Hetty, Cnewr Pansy, Cnewr Purity and Cnewr Verity. The Cnewr ponies also became successful in the showring. Of the mares registered in Volume 1, Sally, a black mare foaled in 1892, had won a first prize at Brecon Show in 1897; the cream mare Princess, foaled in 1885, also won a first prize at Brecon in 1897; and the grey Empress, foaled in 1894, won a first at Defynock and second at Hay in 1901.

There had been ponies at Cnewr before these, and in 1909 Robert (Junior) wrote to his uncle Thomas in Scotland to try to ascertain the pedigree of Cnewr Jack. This was a very influential stallion, foaled at Cnewr in 1867, and winner of a Silver Medal at Brecon Show in 1869 presented by Howel Gwyn Esq. of Buckland. Robert received the pedigree of Cnewr Jack as sired by Cnewr Black and White out of Cnewr Panty by Trotting Lion, but accompanying the reply were the rather pessimistic comments:

With regard to the pedigree of ponies do you really think that it is worth troubling about. What good is it going to do. Do you imagine that you are going to get better prices for those that are sold and where are those fine foreigners coming from with plenty of money in their pocket to buy them. The days of ponydom are over. They have served their age and generation, but they are no longer required for general usefulness but are only serviceable in wild barren districts where roads don't exist. Other motive power, Steam, Electricity & Petrol have recently taken the place of animals for travelling over the roads and a few years more few horses of any kind will be wanted except in the country district. No flesh and blood can compete with machines. Just look at the difference in speed of motor car or cycle on a good road to that of a horse. The one thing I can see to help your pony trade would be to ship three-fourths of them to some country where land is worth nothing e.g. Patagonia and where there would be no chance of them coming back.

There is no record of three-quarters of the Cnewr ponies being shipped to Patagonia and, fortunately for present-day breeders, Thomas McTurk's prophesy of 'days of ponydom are over' has not materialised!

Cnewr ponies in 1987 on the hills overlooking the Cray Reservoir. (*Photo: Desda Hone*)

It is sad that, while the ponies continued to be bred in large numbers at Cnewr, for economic reasons their registrations were not recorded in the WSB. At this time there was close collaboration between the Cnewr and Forest Studs. For example, one of Mr Miller's earlier sires was Rapid Roan, a dark brown roan foaled in 1898, bred at Cnewr and sired by Pompey. However, while the Forest ponies continued to be registered within the WSB (thereby enabling Mr Miller to benefit from the export trade, with 19 Forest ponies exported to the USA in 1912), the registrations of the Cnewr ponies lapsed for 40 years.

Robert McTurk (junior) died in 1942. He had never married and the present owners are the descendants of his sister Elizabeth and his brother Thomas. The estate was run by his executors until incorporated into the Cnewr Estate Company in 1957. Thomas McTurk, who was farming in Dumfries, took over the management in 1944 and became the first managing director of the company.

Criban Cockade, son of the famous Criban Socks, was purchased to run out with the Cnewr mares in 1943 and the registrations of all the ponies had to start all over again, the mares being inspected for Foundation Stock registration in the Appendix of the Stud Book. Again, one generation of up-grading was lost, the daughters of Criban Cockade being registered as FS, whereas if their dams had been registered as FS the Cockade daughters would have been FS1, thus saving one generation.

A draft sale of Cnewr ponies was held in 1947 where prices were not too high, apart from Criban Cockade for whom Mr Gwyn Price of Blaendyrin had to pay 75 guineas, equivalent to about £1,200 today. Another draft sale of 54 ponies was held at Cnewr on 4 November 1954, where the majority were FS daughters of Criban Cockade with a few FS1 daughters of these mares sired by Criban Pilot, Coed Coch Sadyrnin, Clan Bard or Bolgoed Squire. I remember buying two ten-year-old mares there, Cnewr Jess and Cnewr Belle, for 29 and 20 guineas respectively. These mares had previously only rarely seen any humans. Buying them was easy, getting them home and dealing with them at the other end was the problem. Cnewr Belle was sold on, and Cnewr Jess stayed with us until her death but never allowed herself to be handled. Another FS daughter of Criban Cockade on the 1954 sale was the cream Cnewr Beauty; bought by Mr Emrys Griffiths she eventually went to Mrs Hone's stud in Monmouth, where her granddaughters now are. Among the FS1 fillies on the sale were Cnewr Moonlight (daughter of Cnewr Belle), which went to Llanarth Stud, and Cnewr Marvel and Cnewr Black Beauty, which proved their worth as good breeders at Synod Stud. Cnewr Marvel won a third prize at the 1959 Royal Welsh Show for Synod Stud and went on to breed Tydi Gem, dam of

Synod Gem who in turn is dam of the 1990 Royal Welsh Section C first prize-winning yearling colt Synod Gabriel.

Two influential stallions used at Cnewr in the 1970s were Revel Brandy (who was sold at a West Wales sale for a record figure) and Cui Maestro, who has been in great demand as a sire at many major studs, for example, Gredington.

There were two further reduction sales in 1968 and 1982, and interest at Cnewr seemed guaranteed under the managing director Mr David Lloyd (grandson of Elizabeth McTurk). The stud secured valuable outcrosses at the 1978 Coed Coch Dispersal Sale in the form of the five-year-old Coed Coch Heddwen (700 guineas), the four-year-old Coed Coch Orgraff (550 guineas) and the yearling Coed Coch Einir (400 guineas).

Therefore it was very sad to learn in 1987 that after 125 years of pony breeding at Cnewr, the stud of 43 ponies was to be dispersed on 2 October. Sinton Solomon, who had been senior sire for so many years at Cnewr and was then aged 27, was not in the auction but was given back to his breeder, Mrs Joan Bullock, who allowed him to live at Bengad Stud until his death in 1990. The two mares who received most attention were Cnewr Sylvia (bay, by Revel Brandy) and Cnewr Telstar

Cnewr Sylvia, top-priced mare at the 1987 Cnewr dispersal sale. (*Photo: Richard Miller*)

(black, by Cui Maestro), and they sold for 520 and 500 guineas respectively. The top price of the sale was 800 guineas, paid by Mrs Farrow of the Waitwith Stud (breeder of the 1990 Royal Welsh Show champion Waitwith Romance) for a two-year-old chestnut filly, Cnewr Delyth, daughter of Sinton Solomon from a mare called Ronen Thursa by Rowfant Seal.

## Forest Stud

A founder member of the WPCS in 1902, member of Council for Breconshire and one of the five members of the Editing Committee, was Mr William Stevenson Miller of Forest Lodge, Brecon. Mr Miller, the son of an Ayrshire farmer, was born in 1843 and married in 1869. He came to Wales to rent Forest Lodge (comprising then some 1,500 acres) in 1875, about 20 years after the other Scot, Mr McTurk, had come to Cnewr, both farms having been part of the same Great Forest Crown Property from the year 1093 until 1815 (Commons Act). Mr Miller soon became the biggest sheep farmer in Breconshire, renting another three farms – Trebinchen, Treberffyd and Carfartha – and employing eight shepherds and three waggoners, all of whom lived in cottages adjoining the farm, forming a small community of their own.

Mr Miller was the biggest owner (4 stallions and 46 mares) in Volume 1 of the WSB. To begin with the 'Forest' prefix was not adopted, and the stallions were named Black Prince, Brown Prince and Christopher Scott, all foaled in 1899, and Rapid Roan (foaled in 1898) which had been bought from Cnewr. One mare had the strange name of 'Enoch', since she had been bred by Enoch Williams of Glwydfawr, Sennybridge! Another mare, Jewel (foaled in 1886), had won first prizes at Devynock Show in 1889, 1890 and 1900. A black mare named Queen, bred by T. Williams of Llanwern, Brecon in 1894 and sired by Cnewr Jack, won first prizes at Brecon County Shows in 1897 and 1901. Of the 50 ponies registered in Volume 1, 17 were blacks, 12 browns, 9 bays, 6 chestnuts, 3 roans, and one each were grey, dun and palomino.

By Volume 11 of the WSB (1912) Mr Miller had registered 48 stallions and 259 mares. They were mostly sired by Forest Adbolton Sir Horace, Forest Mountain Model and Forest Klondyke, Mr Miller having added the 'Forest' prefix when he bought the stallions. Klondyke was bred by my great-grandmother's brother John Thomas of Tre'rddol in 1894, and was sold to Mr Miller for £100 after winning the championship at the 1905 Welsh National Show. Adbolton Sir Horace, foaled in

Mr W. S. Miller (1843–1928), owner of the greatest number of ponies of any single owner in Volume 1 of the Welsh Stud Book.

1899, stood at 13 hands 3 in., and Mr Miller's intention was to breed smart harness ponies sired by him. Forest Mountain Model was a dark chestnut stallion, foaled in 1900 and standing at 12 hands. He had both parents registered in the Hackney Stud Book, his sire being Sir Gibbie and his dam Humph II, who is quoted as having been sold to the USA for a record price of 320 guineas. Mountain Model was bred by W. W. Rycroft of Park Drive, Bradford, Yorkshire.

We have seen Mrs Olive Tilford Dargan's description in her 1913 book *The Welsh Pony* of how she saw 200 'Forest' ponies grazing on a Sunday morning near Brecon (*see p. 40 above*). When 116 Welsh ponies were exported to the USA in 1912, 19 of them were from Forest. In Volume 2 of the Stud Book of the Welsh Pony and Cob Society of America (1911–12), there are recorded 10 Forest stallions and 42 Forest mares. Tom Morgan, who had worked with them at Forest Lodge, was persuaded to travel with them to the USA to show them for their new owners, and he stayed there until the outbreak of war in 1914 when he came back to Wales to enlist. Unfortunately, registrations of the progeny of American imported Welsh ponies of this period were not kept up, and they do not appear in the later American Stud Books.

Draft sales of Forest ponies were held regularly at Brecon market, with Mr Miller often officiating as auctioneer, having founded the auctioneering firm of

Thomas and Miller. With his Scottish connections Mr Miller easily established a good market for his ponies in the north. Each September a waggonload consisting mostly of three-year-old geldings would leave Brecon railway station for Lanark Sale, where they usually sold for between 30 and 80 guineas, which was considerable money in those days. Some of 'Hackney' type sold for harness work in the cities, for example, for doctors and tradesmen, others of a more 'Cobby' type were sold to work in the pits. Many thousands of ponies were sold every year off the Welsh hills to work underground.

The Forest ponies formed the foundation for many later studs such as Revel and Bowdler. The Criban ponies also intermingled with Forest ponies, Criban Socks having been bred at Forest Lodge, using a Criban stallion (Criban Shot) on a Forest mare (Criban) Forest Lass (foaled in 1918), great-granddaughter of Old Cwmclyn, a mare bred by Mr Miller in 1888.

Criban Socks, bred at Forest. A winner of many championships, she is the 'almost perfect' model taken to represent the breed on the present-day WPCS car sticker.

Mr and Mrs Miller had three daughters, Lily, Helen and Jessie, and it would be Jessie who often went with the exodus of sheep and ponies from Forest Lodge for winter 'tack' to Cardiganshire or the Gower, travelling an average of 20 miles a day and putting up for the night at various farms with grazing for the sheep and unhandled ponies.

Mr Miller was a very kindly man who would often help neighbouring Welsh farmers who were ill or in trouble. Devout Presbyterians, the Millers drove every Sunday to the English chapel at Brecon. Mr Miller also gave great service to the county of Brecon, being elected Chairman of the County Council at the age of seventy-seven in 1920. Mrs Miller died in 1923 and was buried in the Welsh Presbyterian chapel in Libanus.

The last draft sale of Forest ponies took place at Brecon market in 1924, and after sending off a load of ponies to Scotland in 1926 there were only very few left at Forest Lodge. Mr Miller continued his public work until he was eighty-five years old. In 1928 he became ill and died on 7 July and was buried beside his wife at Libanus.

## Criban, Cui and Criban (R) Studs

A founder member of the WPCS in 1902 was Mr Howell William Richards of Abercriban, Coed Hir and Ystrad. These three farms lie in the valley of Taffechan on the south of the Brecon Beacons, the highest of the mountains stretching from Abergavenny in the east and incorporating the Black Mountains as far as Brynaman in the west.

The Richards family had farmed this area for over 300 years. H. W. Richards, born in 1865, was a descendant of Howell ap Richard, born at Coed Hir in 1697. Eight Mountain pony mares were registered in Volume 1 of the WSB: Black Bess (foaled in 1890) and her daughter Black Bess II (foaled in 1897), Ystrad Jewel (foaled in 1893) and her daughter Roanie (foaled in 1897), Vaynor Duchess (foaled in 1897) and her daughter Vaynor Duchess II (foaled in 1900), Beacon Lass (foaled in 1900) and Torpantau Belle (foaled in 1895). Thus it is seen that no one particular prefix was adopted at this time but rather several prefixes, depending on which mountain the ponies inhabited, such as Vaynor, Torpantau or Ystrad. Mr and Mrs Richards and their four children at this time lived at Abercriban, where they stayed until 1915, when the Water Board flooded the farmhouse with much of its good farming land and the little Taffechan church to form a reservoir for Merthyr Tydfil,

Cardiff, Pontypridd and the Rhondda valleys. Fortunately the grazing rights on the Brecon Beacons were retained by the Richardses and other families who had kept ponies on the Beacons for centuries. A neighbouring farmer was Mr Tom Thomas of Pentreabercanafan, who owned Pentre Bucephalus (foaled in 1906), great grandsire of Criban Shot, and this same family bred Criban Biddy Bronze.

There were hundreds of ponies on the Brecon Beacons in the eighteenth and nineteenth centuries, and records of the Criban ponies go back for over 200 years. Until 1850 these ponies were all bays, blacks, browns, dark chestnuts or occasionally dark duns. Around 1840 Mr Crawshay Bailey of Cyfarthfa Castle, Merthyr Tydfil, allowed his Arab stallion to run with the ponies of the nearby Brecon Beacons. This Arab stallion started the grey strain at Abercriban, for example Gentle Mary (who was never registered since she had died before 1902), and also the grey strain for adjoining Pentreabercanafan, producing Dyoll Moonlight, dam of Dyoll Starlight.

Gentle Mary in 1897 produced Wild Flash, who was registered in Volume 11 (1912) of the WSB, and her daughter (foaled in 1905), the pony which the Richards family drove for many years, was registered as Vaynor Flash. Vaynor Flash was a very fast pony and few Breconshire ponies could pass her on the road; under saddle in 1907 she won the Breconshire Coronation Racing Cup! Wild Flash was also the dam of one of the foundation sires, Criban Wild Wonder (foaled in 1918), whose sire was Criban Orion (bred at Pentreabercanafan), whose other son Criban Kid was sire of the famous Criban Shot.

Across the Beacons to the west lived Mr W. S. Miller of Forest Lodge, so the Richardses could also avail themselves of the 'Forest' stallions. In 1906 the two sons, Llewellyn and Dick, rode the two mares Ystrad Jewel and her daughter Roanie over to Forest Lodge to be covered by Klondyke. Jewel duly produced Ystrad Klondyke, whose daughter Criban Chestnut Swell was dam of Criban Shot. By 1910 the Richards family had registered the 'Criban' prefix in the name of Howell William Richards and the three sons, H. Llewellyn Richards, Richard J. Richards and William R. Richards. This partnership continued until 1934 when Dick Richards joined the Ministry of Agriculture and got married to Sheila in Cornwall in 1938, and the youngest son Willie and his wife Betty founded the Cui Stud at Pwllycalch. Mr Richards senior spent most of his life in the saddle shepherding on the Beacons. For some time he was Joint-Master of the Gelligaer Foxhounds, and he won a point-to-point race when he was well over 60 years old. A photograph of Mr Richards Senior appears in Volume 43 of the WSB riding

Mr Howell W. Richards, aged 89 years, with Clan Marshall. (*Photo: Wynne Davies*)

Criban Mog (presented to the King of Nepal) in 1961 when he was 96 years old! He was president of the WPCS for 1938–9 and died in 1963, having been married for 68 years (Mrs Mary Richards died in 1959).

The Richards family did not show their Mountain ponies extensively, as compared with other studs of that period, such as the Dinarth and Grove Studs, which kept grooms exclusively for showing their animals all over Britain. However, Criban Shot (foaled in 1920) won prizes locally at Bedwellty and Devynock before winning the Royal Welsh medal in 1924, and was later (1926) exported to the USA. Criban Socks, the elegant daughter of Criban Shot, was foaled in 1926 and again shown locally, winning at the Bath and West Show (Cardiff) in 1936 where she was sold to Dinarth Hall. After this she won extensively all over Britain.

In 1937 Llewellyn and Rene Richards lived at Oundle in Northamptonshire and had concentrated on producing riding ponies, having crossed some of the Mountain ponies with a top-class polo pony Silverdale Bowtint, but they also kept some purebred Mountain ponies at Oundle. By 1937 numbers at Oundle and Talybont-on-Usk (where Mr Richards senior moved after Abercriban was flooded) had increased to such large numbers that an auction sale was arranged. On 7 May 1937

Criban Shot at the 1924 Royal Welsh Show held by Mr Dick Richards, Mr Llewellyn Richards behind.

40 ponies from Oundle and 50 ponies from Talybont-on-Usk were offered. Prices were not very high that year, and included amongst the ponies sold were Tregoyd Starlight (Royal Welsh Show champion in 1949) at 10½ guineas; Grove Wampa (of complete Mathrafal breeding: Mathrafal Wampus x Mathrafal Ritaway), who went on to produce Revel Wampus in 1938 and Revel Bluebird (noted sire in USA) in 1940, fetched 17½ guineas. Withdrawn at 7 guineas was Criban Sunray (who later that year was sold to Farnley Farms, USA, where she became a very famous foundation mare) and at 8 guineas Criban Rachel, who went on to produce some of the best ponies for Cui Stud, including Cui Spark, Emperor, Sunset, Rachel, Mary and Rose, and then sold for 30 guineas to Dyrin Stud on the 1952 Criban sale.

After the second war interest in ponies was on the increase again. Mr Llewellyn Richards had moved back to his native Talybont-on-Usk and was living at Pontsti-cill, where he had bred sufficient ponies to warrant another sale of 44 ponies, which was held on 5 November (Brecon Fair Day) 1946. Top price of the sale, 50 guineas, was paid by Captain Brierley for the eight-year-old stallion Revel Wampus. The same buyer also bought the stallion Criban Historical (30 guineas) and the mares Criban Ensa and Criban White Wings at 40 and 33 guineas respectively. Criban Rally, daughter of the famous Criban Socks, was sold to Ceulan at 33 guineas and her typey little son Criban Atom was bought by Major Careless for 28 guineas. Mr John Berry paid what was then a record price for a filly foal (Criban Golden Spray) of 20 guineas. This was generally regarded to be a very good sale which gave much needed encouragement to the Mountain pony breeders of Wales.

The last Criban sale of 65 ponies was held on 2 May 1952, when far-and-away the highest price (139 guineas) was paid for the roan yearling colt Hinton Beacon (Gaerstone Beacon x Criban Posy) who, apart from siring a few for Mrs Somervell of the Plumgarths Stud, was not much heard of. The two very famous stallions Criban Bantam (Bolgoed Shot Star x Criban Brenda) and Vardra Sunstar (reserve champion at the 1951 Royal Welsh Show: Criban Pebble x Vardra Charm) sold for 70 and 74 guineas respectively to Mr Gwyn Price of Dyrin and Mr Tom Parry of Gurnos. Other noted animals included in this sale were Criban Opera (76 guineas), Criban Red Chip (40 guineas to Mrs Pennell), Criban Activity (winner of the Royal Welsh Show ridden class trophy outright, 48 guineas to Cusop Stud), and Criban

Criban Fay, winner of championships initially for Criban Stud, then for Glanusk and Ceulan Studs, here shown by Wynne Davies.

Topsy (winner of WPCS Championship medal at Brecon in 1951, 66 guineas to Miss Horton).

With Mr and Mrs Llewellyn Richards living at the Allt, Talybont-on-Usk, and having lost considerable grazing for forestry and reservoirs, the pony numbers were reduced. However, many champions still emerged, and two which did well for me were Criban Fay and Criban Pep, both foaled in 1957 and both sired by Gredington Ianto.

Criban ponies also formed the foundation of successful studs overseas. The two bay mares Criban Miriam (foaled in 1961), descended from the original Black Bess, and Criban Bar Belle (foaled in 1958), daughter of Bowdler Brewer, were both exported to Denmark in 1963 to start the Welsh Society in that country. Pony breeding in New Zealand was given a big boost by the export in 1965 of three ponies from Criban to their nephew David Coxhead of Timaru: the stallion Revel Consul, the mare Criban Old China, and the yearling filly Criban Fair Frills. Criban Old China (foaled in 1962) represented the best Criban bloodlines, since her dam was Criban Old Gold (foaled in 1953 by Criban Cockade, son of Criban Socks) out of Criban Mair (foaled in 1949 by Owain Glyndwr) out of Criban Snow White (foaled in 1946 by Bolgoed Sqire) out of Criban Eve (foaled in 1936 by Mathrafal Tuppence) out of Criban Betsy (foaled in 1920 by Criban Kid, also sire of Criban Shot) out of Criban Bess (foaled in 1912 by Ystrad Klondyke) out of Black Bess II (foaled in 1897) out of Black Bess (foaled in 1890) – which is where the story began.

Mr Llewellyn Richards judged at the Royal Welsh Show in 1966 and in most overseas countries, including Australia in 1979 when he was 85 years old. He rode his Cob Virginian at Brecon Show in 1978, was president of the WPCS in 1959–60 and member of Council for over 50 years, and all Welsh pony breeders throughout the world mourned his death on 7 May 1982.

His youngest brother Willie of Cui Stud predeceased him in 1954, which resulted in a dispersal sale of 150 ponies on 1 October 1954. Highest priced stallion at this sale was the old-fashioned Gaerstone Beacon (44 guineas), who went to the Pendock Stud where he became a very important sire. Pendock Stud also bought the yearling filly Cui Flora (54 guineas), who later was dam of such well-known ponies as Pendock Pilleth, Honeysuckle and Periwinkle. Cui Metal was a much-admired mare, who was sold to Miss Horton for 50 guineas. She became a big show winner and was exported through Ceulan Stud to Mrs Mohler in the USA in 1957. Another Cui mare on the sale which went to the USA from Ceulan was Cui Moon Flicker (25 guineas); her dam, Cui Blue Moon, was also in the sale and fetched 36 guineas. Cui June, dam of Blue Moon, was wisely bought back by Willie's widow Mrs Betty Richards, as was her daughter Cui April, and April became the foundation mare for Mrs Betty Richards. Cui June's filly foal was also wisely retained. She was Cui Melody, granddam of Cui Mi'Lord that was used very successfully at Ceulan for four years after which, when his daughters came of breeding age, he was sold to Denmark. His grandson Waxwing Herod was top sire in Australia in 1988 and 1989. Another 12 Cui mares were exported to the USA in 1957 followed by 10 in 1958. The mares Cui Pancake, Cui Merry May, Cui Jean and Cui Gay Girl were amongst the original mares exported to Denmark in 1961. Cui ponies are still in

Roundup of Cui ponies. The hill ponies are rounded up annually at the time of weaning of the foals.

83

good demand at the Fayre Oaks Sales and the Richardses' daughter Sarah also has her own ponies bred under the 'Llanfigan' prefix.

At the 1954 Cui Sale, 20 mares were bought by Mr and Mrs Dick Richards to start the Criban (R) Stud. Mr Dick Richards had retired from the Ministry of Agriculture after periods in Cornwall, Wiltshire, Cambridge and Northumberland, where he had given much assistance to pony breeding. Sheila continued with her welfare work back in Wales, devoting hours to caring for wild ponies and foals at sales, overseeing their transport and giving them hay and water if they stayed in the saleyard overnight. Dick Richards had a very good eye for a pony, starting from a gift of Roanie (foaled in 1897) which he begged from his father since they were born in the same year! He judged at the 1963 Royal Welsh Show and his services as a judge were in great demand all over Britain and overseas. The Criban (R) ponies became well known in the showring, mainly within Section B, and many were exported. Dick Richards had a host of friends within the pony and sheep-dog trials world and his death in 1975 was a time of great sadness. Mrs Sheila Richards continued with her welfare work until illness forced her to retire in 1989; I consider it a privilege to have given an eulogy to this wonderful lady who died on 28 January 1991 having devoted her later years to the welfare of ponies throughout Wales.

## Stanage Stud, Mynd Stud

Very much at the helm of the formation of the WPCS in 1901 was Mr Charles Coltman Rogers of Stanage Park, Brampton Brian, Herefordshire, the house familiar to television viewers as the residence of the 'Lord of the Manor' in the popular series *Blot on the Landscape*.

Mr Coltman Rogers was a very able gentleman, equally at home reading Latin and Greek as writing about Darwin's theory of evolution. He also rendered great service to the local community as Chairman of the Radnorshire County Council, Stanage Park actually being in Wales though having an English postal address. Mr Coltman Rogers must have spent hours researching Welsh pony and Cob pedigrees of the pre-Stud Book era, and the first five volumes of the WSB contain invaluable genealogies without which there would be no record of the great Welsh ponies and Cobs of the nineteenth century. He would have had to travel the length and breadth of Wales for this information, recording pedigrees which breeders and owners had in their minds but were loathe or perhaps unable to put on paper. Mr Marshall Dugdale of Llwyn was the first chairman of the WPCS, and Mr Coltman

Mr Charles Coltman Rogers.
Researchers into early pedigrees
owe him an immense debt of
gratitude for travelling around
Wales and recording pedigrees
which were published in the
early volumes of the Welsh Stud
Book.

Rogers was vice-chairman, taking over as chairman on the death of Mr Dugdale in 1918. He held this office until his friend Lord Swansea became Chairman in 1927. Mr Coltman Rogers was also vice-president of the WPCS in 1903–4 and president in 1918–19, an office held by his granddaughter, Mrs Teresa Smalley, in 1985–6.

Meticulous records were kept of all the ponies and Cobs at Stanage. Originally the stud concentrated on Cobs, which were sold for £20 to £50 between 1905 and 1926. The records show many of them sold as mounts for soldiers, and others were sold to sire remounts.

For the Mountain ponies the services of the top sires of the day were sought. Stanage Polar Lights, sired by Greylight, was foaled in 1906, followed by Stanage

Stanage Sunrise (foaled 1916 by Bleddfa Shooting Star) at Stanage Park.

Polar Star and Stanage Grey Lady, also by Greylight, in 1907 and 1908. Polar Star was sold as a yearling colt for 18 guineas to Lord Lucas to run in the New Forest. Stanage Halley's Comet, foaled in 1910, was sired by Dyoll Starlight and was later used at stud at Stanage. Stanage Sunrise (foaled in 1916) was sired by the magnificent Bleddfa Shooting Star.

Mr Coltman Rogers exhibited and attended agricultural shows regularly, and the Stanage Stud documents contained detailed records of such stallions as Greylight and Dyoll Starlight accompanied by photographs taken by Muriel A. G. Rogers.

The noted stallion Stanage Daylight was bred by Daniel Price of Llangadog in 1905, from his famous mare Star I by Merlyn Myddfai. He was sold first to T. B. Lewis of Bronallt, Llanwrtyd Wells, and then to Lord Lucas, and he spent some years in the New Forest before being purchased back to Wales by Mr Coltman Rogers. As soon as he returned to his native heath, he was given the Stanage prefix and immediately made his presence felt in the showring, winning 'best pony in the show' at Craven Arms in 1913, first at the Newport Welsh National Show in 1914, first and WPCS medal at the Cardiff RASE Show in 1919, and so on.

Possibly the best of Stanage Daylight's progeny was Stanage Perfect Day, foaled in 1916 out of Stanage Aldernut. He won a second prize at the 1919 Cardiff RASE Show and was sold two months later for £60 to Mr Edward Hirst of the Springmead Stud, Sydney, Australia. Stanage Perfect Day won many prizes at New South Wales shows in 1921, his greatest success being the championship of the Royal Agricultural Society of New South Wales, whose *Journal* contained his photograph along with the following report:

> A pony without ego is a pony without soul. Stanage Perfect Day is all 'ego'. Whether static or kinetic, that is to say, whether posed or in action, he is a beauty. His colour should please Mr Hirst, which is that of the hobby-horse, namely dappled grey. If pony breeding in New South Wales does not receive a fillip, and if the great little varmints themselves don't show strong improvement, it will not be due to any sins of omission on the part of Mr Hirst.

The Stanage ponies went as foundations of many other studs and premium societies. Stanage The Nut (foaled in 1912), another daughter of Stanage Aldernut,

Stanage Perfect Day, foaled in 1916 and exported to Australia in 1919.

was sold to the University College of North Wales for £35 in 1918; Stanage Revelry was sold to the Hon. Mrs L. Brodrick of Coed Coch in 1919; and Stanage Meteor (foaled in 1913) and foal were sold in 1922 to Miss Monica Dunne of Gatley Park, the foal being later registered as Gatley Stardust. She was the dam of Coed Coch Socyn (Stoatley Stud) and Coed Coch Sensigl, who produced so many wonderful champions at Coed Coch including the 1960 Royal Welsh Show Supreme Champion Coed Coch Symwl (Gredington Stud). Stanage Estella (foaled in 1920) was exported to Miss Doris Roberts of the Bowral Stud, Australia in 1925; Stanage Skylight (foaled in 1922) was sold to Lord Swansea as a premium stallion for the Fairwood Association on Gower; and Stanage Planet was sold to E. D. Morgan, Long Island, USA for £26 in 1926, and was stud stallion for many years at Mrs Hope Ingersoll's Grazing Fields Stud, where many of the breeding stock in 1991 traced back to him. Thus the influence of Stanage blood was world-wide.

Mr Coltman Rogers died in the spring of 1930. His eldest son was Guy, whose

Eleven ponies leaving Stanage Park for the 1919 Knighton Show. Their names are recorded on the photograph.

son David was killed in a tragic car accident in 1957. David's son Jonathon and his wife Sophie live at Stanage and are breeding Welsh Cobs under the 'Stanage' prefix.

The younger son of Mr Charles Coltman Rogers was Julian, whose daughter Teresa started the Mynd Stud in 1949 with Mountain ponies, later going on to breed some very influential Section B ponies. Her original Mountain pony mare was Mynd Twilight (foaled in 1944), bought from the Bolgoed Stud and daughter of no less than the illustrious Grove Peep O'Day. The stud stallion used most extensively was the lovely red roan, Criban Rocky, son of Ceulan Revolt out of Criban Nylon, daughter of Criban Heather Bell. Various other bloodlines were brought in such as Rondeels Cavalla, imported from Holland and a big winner both in Holland and in Britain. The Mynd Mountain Pony Stud was dispersed at a joint sale with the Llanerch Stud in 1979.

## Bowdler, Gretton and Gaerstone Studs

Amongst the names of subscribers of one shilling for membership of the Church Stretton (Longmynd) Hill Pony Improvement Society in 1890, 10 years before the formation of the Welsh Pony and Cob Society, was that of Mr George Preece, Hope Bowdler Farm. Mr Preece joined the WPCS in 1904, and Volume 7 of the WSB contains registrations for Bowdler Belle I (foaled in 1897), Bess I (foaled in 1903) and Beauty (also foaled in 1903). Most of the stallions owned or leased by the Longmynd Society at this time were sons of Dyoll Starlight, for example Stretton Torchlight, Stretton Sirocco, Stretton Dynamite and Dyoll Satellite, and gradually the offspring of the original bay and brown Bowdler mares all became greys and possibly lost some of their inherent hardiness. A return to the hardier colours was achieved by using the darker coloured stallions, the bay Mathrafal Havoc (foaled in 1915), the black Mathrafal Rascal (foaled in 1914), the black Forest Jehu (foaled in 1914) and his sire the dark chestnut Forest Mountain Model (foaled in 1900, son of Humph II who was sold to the USA in 1910 for 320 guineas, equivalent to over £10,000 today), and the dark chestnut Forest Klondyke (foaled in 1909), son of the original Klondyke.

George Preece Senior obtained the top price of the 1922 Collective WPCS Sale when he sold Forest Mountain Model for 58 guineas, a feat repeated by George Preece Junior in 1981, when he sold Bowdler Bowstring at the Fayre Oaks Sale to top the Section As at 900 guineas.

George Preece Senior gave up farming in 1941 and a farm sale was held of 556 Kerry Hill sheep, 86 cattle, 10 working horses, 31 pigs, farm implements, two Chevrolet Stock lorries and 20 Welsh Mountain ponies. Fortunately some of the valuable bloodlines were bought by the Preece sons: George, who continued at Hope Bowdler, Frank of Gretton, which is towards Much Wenlock to the east, and Willie of Gaerstone, Gaerstone being the name of a large rock on the end of Bowdler hill overlooking the Longmynd Hills and the town of Church Stretton.

One of the first of the Bowdler ponies to achieve great prominence in the showring was Bowdler Brightlight. Foaled in 1923, he was sired by Mathrafal Havoc out of Bowdler Bounce, daughter of Bowdler Belle IV, who in turn was daughter of the original Bowdler Belle I (foaled in 1897). Bowdler Brightlight was kept on at the stud for 10 years, after which he was sold to Mr Edgar Herbert who showed him at the 1933 Shropshire and West Midland Show. By the time of the Royal Welsh that year, Mr Herbert had sold him to Mr Tom Wood-Jones, and Brightlight spent most of 1933 and 1934 at Ceulan. At the 1933 Royal Welsh, Brightlight distinguished himself by beating the elegant Grove Will o' the Wisp to stand second to the unbeatable Grove Sprightly. Amongst his progeny during that period in Mid-Wales was the Cob-type stallion Teifi Brightlight I. By 1935 Brightlight had become the property of Dinarth Hall, for whom he was very successful until the owner's death, and he was sold for 45 guineas at the Dinarth Hall Dispersal Sale in October 1937 to Mrs Sivewright, who lived in the New Forest. He did not stay very long with Mrs Sivewright before going on to his final home at Farnley Farm in the USA, where he joined Bowdler Brownie (exported there in 1937) and was one of the top US sires until his death in 1949.

Brightlight's most influential son left at Bowdler was Bowdler Blue Boy, premium stallion at Church Stretton for 1936–9 and 1952–4, and widely used outside Bowdler, for example at Craven and Brierwood Studs. Best known of Blue Boy's 'Bowdler' progeny are the two full brothers and their full sister: the 1961 Royal Welsh Show champion Bowdler Brewer; Bowdler Blighter, premium stallion at Aber hills, Revel and Gurnos; and a throw-back to her bay ancestors, the elegant Bowdler Belle, a well-known winner during the years 1955–8.

In 1955 Frank Preece decided to sell up his Welsh Mountain pony herd of 13 mares, 10 foals, 4 yearling fillies and 8 young colts and retired to Lawley View, where he died in 1989. His brothers Willie and George decided that the sale would be a good opportunity to reduce their stock, adding 4 stallions, 5 mares and foals from Gaerstone and 4 stallions and 4 mares and foals from Bowdler, which along with a few geldings made up an exciting sale of 70 ponies. The first two mares on the sale, Gretton Sunset and Gretton Suncloud, two very nice daughters of Bowdler Butterfly, were secured for Mr Tolan of the USA for 98 and 85 guineas. Three other Gretton mares were bought for the USA, Miss Brodrick buying Gretton Sunstar and Gretton Flash for 47 and 50 guineas for Mrs Mackay-Smith, and Gretton Sunbeam for Mr George Fernley. Gretton Charm was the best of the yearling fillies. Bowdler Blighter, who later became a very influential sire throughout Wales, was sold for 50 guineas to Mr Tom Parry of the Gurnos Stud, Merthyr Tydfil.

Possibly the best known of the Gaerstone ponies was Gaerstone Beacon, a sturdy roan stallion, foaled in 1944. Sired by Bowdler Brilliant out of Bowdler Betty by

Bowdler Blue Boy (*left*) with Mr George Preece winning the Church Stretton premium stallion show in 1937, from Longmynd Hyperion (Mr T. Roberts), Bowdler Banker (Mr Dai Howe), Quicksilver (Mr T. Andrews), Stanage Skylight (Mr J. Downes). (*Photo courtesy of Mrs Sommerville*)

Stanage Daylight, he had spent several years at the Cui Stud and was sold in 1954 to the Pendock Stud where he then stayed to end his days. It was a shock to Welsh pony breeders to learn of the death of Willie, the youngest of the Preece brothers, in 1974, his 44 Gaerstone ponies having been sold by auction at Craven Arms in October 1970.

George Preece often included drafts to sell at the annual Fayre Oaks Sale, and in 1981 when he was approaching his 80th birthday, his consignment of 12 mares and 6 filly foals created much interest. These ponies had never been touched by human hand, let alone trimmed and groomed for selling! Despite their unkempt state they found good trade, with the grey mare Bowdler Bowstring fetching the equal top price for Section As of the whole sale (900 guineas) to Mr Ifor Lloyd of Derwen Stud, who also bought the bay Bowdler Biscuit for 650 guineas. A few Bowdler ponies were then included on every Fayre Oaks Sale until 1984, when 30 ponies were offered for sale at Hereford on 18 December, leaving only two or three at Bowdler. Top price of the 1984 sale was 400 guineas, paid for Bowdler Buttee, a small, old-fashioned fourteen-year-old mare.

Mr George Preece with Bowdler Badger Boy just off to Australia in 1974.

George Preece was elected president of the WPCS for 1976–7, which coincided with his fiftieth wedding anniversary, and he died in February 1987 in his 85th year. His daughter, Miss Mary Preece, still keeps a few mares, so the Bowdler prefix still appears on a very much reduced scale on Fayre Oaks Sales.

## Caer Beris Stud

The person largely responsible for the setting up of the improvement society on the Gower peninsula in 1909 was the Hon. Odo Vivian, President of the Gower Pony Association. He had joined the WPCS in 1905 and was elected vice-president for 1906–7, while living at Glanrafon, Sketty, Swansea. His sister, Miss D. C. Vivian of Clyne Castle, Swansea, was also a member of the WPCS, joining in 1912, and they both had ponies on the Gower common, being two of the many breeders using the 'Fairwood' prefix. The Hon. Odo Vivian was also vice-president of the WPCS in 1914–15; by then he was living at Glanogwr, Bridgend, but there were also ponies kept at the Caer Beris estate in Builth Wells (a timber-framed neo-Jacobean house on the site of a twelfth-century motte) and the photograph of the premium stallion judging on the Eppynt in 1917 (*p. 30*) shows the Caer Beris Stud groom Jack Roberts exhibiting one of their stallions.

The main influence on the Caer Beris ponies was achieved with the purchase in 1920 of a colt, bred by Mrs Greene of the Grove in 1917 but registered in 1919 as Pistyll King Cole, owned by David Davies and Son of the Blaenpistyll Stud in Cardigan. David Davies and Son of Blaenpistyll were life members of the WPCS in 1913, and the son, David Lewis Davies, was elected an honorary life vice-president at the age of 96 years at the 1991 WPCS AGM. When Pistyll King Cole was purchased by the Hon. Odo Vivian his name was changed to Caer Beris King Cole. This was a very shrewd purchase on which to base the Caer Beris Stud; the sire was none other than the noted Grove King Cole II, a stallion who had swept the board in yearling classes in 1912 and gone on to be reserve champion at Shrewsbury in 1913, reserve champion at the NPS, first at the RASE in 1914, reserve champion at the NPS and RASE in 1915, 1916 and 1917, champion at the 1920 NPS Show, and so on.

Dam of Caer Beris King Cole was Grove Sprite II, perhaps more famous as the dam of the illustrious Grove Sprightly. Her dam was the little chestnut mare Grove Fairy, which had been bred on the Gower by William Jones of Sandy Lane, Parkmill. King Cole was mated to the Fairwood mares, producing among others

93

Caer Beris King Cole. Foundation of the Caer Beris Stud and well-known winner in the years 1927–30.

Caer Beris Diamond in 1922, out of Fairwood Dazzle (later re-registered as Caer Beris Dazzle), daughter of Bryngwili Brightlight (by Dyoll Starlight); and Caer Beris Donovan, also foaled in 1922, out of Fairwood Fairy Light by Sparklight (one of the famous full brothers and sisters bred by Daniel Price of Llangadog, by Dyoll Starlight out of Star I).

By 1923 the Hon. Odo Vivian had succeeded to the title of the Third Baron Swansea and was living at Caer Beris. The local pony improvement societies benefited greatly from the loan of high-class stallions. Examples are the two previously mentioned stallions Caer Beris Diamond and Caer Beris Donovan. They were both among the 10 stallions awarded premiums at the 1926 premium judging on Eppynt (Cwmowen Inn), where the judges reported '32 stallions presented and not a poor one amongst them'. Caer Beris Imaway, foaled in 1927 by Caer Beris King Cole out of Mathrafal Ritaway, is regarded by many to have been the most successful stallion of the dozens who served their time on the Longmynd hills, Church Stretton. The Caer Beris ponies won many showring awards all over Britain, Caer Beris King Cole and Caer Beris Dazzle (joined by Clumber Miss Mary, owned by the Misses May and Summers) winning the Garnett Cup for the best group of native ponies of any breed at the 1929 National Pony Show in London.

94

The silver statuette of Caer Beris King Cole competed for annually at the Gower Show, presented by the Hon. Mrs Douglas in memory of her brother Lord Swansea, Third Baron. (*Photo: Wynne Davies*)

Lord Swansea, the Third Baron, was Chairman of Council of the WPCS from 1927 to 1932, representing the important period for the setting up of the present-day Section B. Ill-health caused him to resign from the Chair in 1932 and he died in 1934. A silver memorial statuette of Caer Beris King Cole, competed for annually at the Gower Show, is inscribed: 'Presented by the Hon. Mrs Douglas in memory of her brother Odo Richard Vivian, DSO, MVO, TD, JP, DL, 3rd Baron Swansea, founder of the Fairwood and Pengwern Pony Societies in 1902.' On the other side are engraved some of the winnings of Caer Beris King Cole, such as first Royal Welsh 1927, first RASE 1928, and second National Pony Show 1929.

Lord Swansea, Fourth Baron, resurrected the Caer Beris Stud for the seven years 1958 to 1965. His mares, some of which were descended from the Caer Beris bloodlines of his late father, were Revel Rainbow, Pendock Trinket, Maescwm May Bud, Lower Cwm Fern and Reeves Coral. A very 'big gun' was added to the stud by the purchase of the two-year-old colt Coed Coch Siglen Las (at 700 guineas) at the 1959 Coed Coch Sale, and he soon went on to win prizes for Caer Beris. He

Winners of the Garnett Cup for the best group of native ponies at the 1929 National Pony Show in London: (*left*) Caer Beris King Cole and (*right*) Caer Beris Dazzle (held by stud groom Jack Roberts), both owned by Lord Swansea, and (*centre*) Clumber Miss Mary. (*Photo courtesy of Mrs Ingersoll, USA*)

stood second to Twyford Grenadier at the 1960 Royal Welsh Show, beating Coed Coch Salsbri who had been retained at Coed Coch.

Welsh Mountain pony enthusiasts were sad when the stud which was proving so successful was dispersed. Siglen Las (sold for 550 guineas), six mares and some foals were sold at the 1964 Fayre Oaks Sale. Siglen Las went on to win championships at the 1965 and 1966 Royal Welsh Shows for his new owner Miss Rosey Russell-Allen.

The last foal to be bred at Caer Beris (in 1965) was Caer Beris Rondo, sired by Coed Coch Siglen Las out of Revel Rainbow, but many breeders took advantage of these exceptional bloodlines. For example, Lisvane Stud bred many good ponies out of Caer Beris Crystal (foaled in 1960), daughter of Criban Atom and Reeves Coral.

# Grove Stud

When Mrs Harriet Greene joined the Welsh Pony and Cob Society in 1906 and established the Grove Stud, she had the advantage of unlimited funds. Her father, Mr John Jones of the Grove Estate of over 4,000 acres in Craven Arms, Shropshire, was one of the Directors of the London City and Midland Bank. He died in 1885. Harriet, the only child, married Mr H. D. Greene KC, whose father was a Director of the Bank of England. Mr Greene was Conservative Member of Parliament for Shropshire from 1892 to 1906. Mrs Greene was an accomplished horsewoman, hunting seldom less than three days a week with the Ludlow and other local packs, and she had a very good eye for all types of horses and ponies.

Mrs Greene was a member of the Polo Pony Stud Book Society when it was founded in 1893. She registered three mares in Volume 1 of its Stud Book, published in 1894, including the first mare ever registered: Abbess, number 1, a brown 13 hands 2 in. mare sired by a Thoroughbred; Fidget, number 79, an aged brown mare, height 12 hands, sire unknown, dam Shetland pony; and Lady Help, number 143, foaled 1886, height 14 hands 2 in., of unknown parentage.

Mrs Greene's first registered Welsh pony was Dyoll Ballistite, registration number 151. A grey Mountain pony colt, he was foaled in 1903 and sired by Dyoll Starlight out of Dyoll Bala Gal, a little brown mare bred on Gwastadrhos Common, near Bala. Ballistite had been shown by his breeder Mr Meuric Lloyd at the Welsh National Show in 1906, where the judge, Mr W. S. Miller of Forest Lodge, had placed him fifth behind Mr Evan Jones's Greylight, Mr E. Williams's Montgomery George, Mr Arthur Pughe's Gwyndy Cymro, and Mr Evan Jones's Brigand, another son of Starlight's bred by Mr Lloyd. Mr Lloyd offered Ballistite for sale at an auction held at Llangadog in 1906 and Mrs Greene bought him for 36 guineas. Mrs Greene re-registered him as Grove Ballistite and he had a new registration number of 200.

Mrs Greene did not waste any time enrolling the services of a groom and Ballistite was soon winning major awards in the showring, such as the WPCS championship medal at the 1908 Shropshire and West Midland Show. Ballistite's achievements encouraged Mrs Greene to get two more sons of Dyoll Starlight from Mr Meuric Lloyd, and in 1909 she bought Dyoll (Grove) King Cole for £50 and Dyoll (Grove) Rainbow (full-brother to Ballistite) for £45.

In addition to the stallions, Mrs Greene bought 30 or 40 mares and her build-up of the Grove Stud coincided with the exciting boom to America. During 1911 three

Grove stallions and 20 mares were exported to the USA, followed by six stallions and 24 mares in 1912 and 16 mares in 1913. Grove King Cole was probably the best of the animals to be exported and he was allowed to go since, in 1910, he had sired Grove King Cole II. This was probably the best quality and most spectacular mover of all the hundreds of ponies bred at Grove, and he remained there until the final dispersal sale in June 1927. Another good stallion exported in 1912 was Grove Starlight (a son of Ballistite), who went to His Highness the Maharajah of Alwar, KCSI, India.

The show string had also increased dramatically. In 1912 prizes were won by the stallions Grove Arclight (WPCS medal at Llanwrtyd Wells), Grove Ballistite (WPCS medal at the RASE Show), Grove King Cole II, Grove Rushlight (WPCS medal at Craven Arms), Grove Stallactite (WPCS medal at Church Stretton), and the mares Grove Dazzle, Grove Dolly, Grove Dusky Mite, Grove Limelight (WPCS female medal at Llanwrtyd), Grove Myrtle (WPCS medal at Islington), Grove Snowflake, Grove Sprite, Grove Startle, Grove Sunshine and Nantyrharn Starlight (WPCS female medal, Church Stretton).

The Welsh Mountain pony stallion class at the 1914 Royal Lancashire Show, Liverpool: (*right to left*) Grove Ballistite (*first*), Grove King Cole II, Grove Footlight (all owned by Mrs H. D. Greene), Hawddgar Mountain Chief, Gwyndy Comet, Stanage Daylight. (*Photo: Geo. Toulmin and Sons, Preston*)

The Grove grooms were easily recognised since they all had to be turned out immaculately wearing red waistcoats. Jimmy Wakefield was the senior groom and he went to Lady Wentworth's stud after 1927. Assistant groom was Archie Cook, formerly stud groom at Tanyrallt, who also went to the Wentworth Stud where he showed the Arabs and the Welsh ponies. Afterwards he became stud groom at Mrs Vaughan-Williams's stud in Dorking, and spent his last years in Cardiganshire near Llyn Eiddwen.

War clouds were gathering in 1914 which stopped the export trade and by now 35 stallions and 187 mares had been registered with the Grove prefix. After war was declared on 4 August it was decided to hold a reduction sale, and on 30 September 78 Welsh Mountain ponies of the best bloodlines in Britain, including some prizewinners, were sold by auction at the Home Farm.

In 1913 Mrs Greene had leased the great Dyoll Starlight himself and had outstanding foals by him in 1914 such as Grove Lightheart, daughter of Bleddfa Tell Tale who was also dam of Stallactite, Twilight and King Cole II. The most famous of all the Bleddfa ponies was Bleddfa Shooting Star, bred by Mr Wilmot of

Grove Lightheart, who made 55 guineas with her filly foal at the 1927 dispersal sale. (*Welsh Pony and Cob Stud Book Vol. 23*)

Alveston near Bristol (whose granddaughter Mrs Sally St George is breeding Welsh ponies in Co. Kilkenny, Eire). He was sired by Dyoll Starlight out of Alveston Belle and was sold by Bleddfa to Sir Walter Gilbey, who had a famous stud of Hackneys at Elsenham Hall in Essex. In Sir Walter's ownership, Shooting Star became the idol of the showring, winning championships galore. Sir Walter died in 1914 and despite the war, Mrs Greene bought Shooting Star for 240 guineas at the Elsenham Dispersal in January 1915. Shooting Star was included in the 1916 Grove Stud card (at a stud fee of 2 guineas), listing all his winnings with Sir Walter in 1906–12 and at Newcastle Emlyn (when leased to Llwyncadfor in 1913 and 1914),

Grove Will o' the Wisp, foaled in 1923 by Bleddfa Shooting Star out of Grove Twilight. One of the best Welsh Mountain ponies of all time, he was exported to Italy in 1938. (*Photo from NPS Stud Book, 1937–9, p. 272, courtesy of Abery*)

and his championships while at Grove in 1915: at Islington, the RASE at Nottingham, and Llanrwst.

Also at stud in 1916 were Grove Ballistite, Grove King Cole II, the Welsh Cob stallion Grove Welsh Dragon and the Hackney pony Grove Wild Wales. Mrs Greene assisted the formation of pony improvement societies throughout Wales by lending out her top stallions. Ballistite spent 1915 with the Brynamman Society and his progeny, for example Camnant Ballistite 994 and Tawe Valley Ballistite 992, were retained by these societies, thereby availing them of the best bloodlines in Britain.

Despite the war, Mrs Greene did manage to sell off some ponies now and again. The best known of these was Grove Arclight (foaled in 1908), generally regarded as being the best son of Greylight, and his dam was Wedros Gem by Eiddwen Flyer III. Arclight won first prize at the 1914 Welsh National and was champion at the RASE Show the same year, and then in 1915 he was sold for export to Argentina for a reputed £1,000. He was the first Welsh Mountain pony to be exported there.

With numbers at the stud increasing, another sale (of 40 ponies) was held at the Craven Arms Repository on 12 August 1916. Included were the well-known champion mare Grove Limelight, and Grove Fairy (chestnut mare bred on the Gower), dam of three London champions including Grove Sprite II, dam of Grove Sprightly whose record of nine Royal Welsh Show championships has never been equalled.

By now the Grove Stud had a coterie of show ponies which were proving impossible to beat, winning London group championships over all native breeds in 1921 with Bleddfa Shooting Star, Grove King Cole II, Grove Star of Hope and Grove Lightheart, and repeating this achievement again in 1922 with four Grove-bred ponies (King Cole II, Firelight, Fairy Queen and Sprightly), and again in 1923 with King Cole II, Sprightly, Lightheart and Bright Spot.

Mr Greene had died in 1916 and in 1927 Mrs Greene decided to 'call it a day' and disperse her work of 21 years. On 29 June everything was sold apart from the 26-year-old Bleddfa Shooting Star, who stayed on in honoured retirement for four more years and was buried in the animal cemetery near the Grove house. The year 1927 was a sad one for the Welsh Pony and Cob Society, with the dispersal of the Faraam (Mr Ffitch Mason) and Forest Studs (Mr W. S. Miller), and then Grove. A WPCS Council Meeting was held at Grove on the morning of the sale, when Mr Coltman Rogers and Lord Swansea were elected chairman and vice-chairman respectively, and Mr Lyell and Mr T. J. Jones of Dinarth Stud president and president-elect. Everyone was invited to lunch at 12.30 p.m. at a charge of three shillings (returnable to all purchasers of £2 or more!)

Lady Wentworth had bought the lovely Grove Star of Hope privately from Mrs Greene in 1924, and sent 'Captain Dainty' (a pseudonym for her agent who kept riding stables at Windsor) to the sale to buy six of the best ponies. Grove Lightheart was expected to make the top price of the sale; however, Captain Dainty got her for 55 guineas (including a filly foal by Shooting Star) but had to pay 141 guineas for Grove Moonstone. Moonstone turned out to be an expensive purchase since a month later at the Royal Welsh Show at Swansea she was only seventh in a class won by Kittiwake of Dinarth Hall, and Clumber Miss Mary (bought on the Faraam Sale earlier that year for 34 guineas) was third.

Grove Moonstone, winner of the 1924 Shropshire and West Midland Show and 1925 Royal Lancashire show, who made 141 guineas at the 1927 dispersal sale. (*Welsh Pony and Cob Stud Book Vol. 25*)

Lady Wentworth also bought Grove Fairy Queen for 40 guineas and the two champion stallions Grove King Cole II for 130 guineas (he was champion at the Swansea Royal Welsh Show) and Grove Sprightly (purchased in partnership with Mr Tom Jones Evans) for 126 guineas.

And so the Grove Stud was no more but its influence has been phenomenal through such bloodlines as Grove Star of Hope, dam of Winestead Larina (Revel Stud); Grove Madcap, dam of Coed Coch Mefusen, dam of Coed Coch Madog; Grove Sharp Shooter, sire of Coed Coch Seren; Grove Limestone, dam of Touch-stone of Sansaw (Twyford Stud); Grove Peep O'Day (Blanche Stud, Tregoyd Stud and Bolgoed Stud); and so the list goes on and on.

## Coed Coch Stud, Bryndansi Stud

Without doubt the stud which has had the greatest influence ever on Welsh Mountain pony and Welsh Section B breeding is the Coed Coch Stud of Abergele, North Wales, if only for the sheer weight of numbers. At the time of the dispersal sale in September 1978 there were 136 Section As, 84 Section Bs and 24 riding ponies, a grand total of 244 animals of the highest calibre.

The Wynne family of Coed Coch and Trofarth and their kinsmen the Williams-Wynns of Wynnstay and Cefn had been noted horse breeders for several centuries. It was an ancestor of Lt. Col. Edward Williams-Wynn, the last owner of the Coed Coch Stud, who was alleged to have turned the Thoroughbred stallion Merlin out on the Ruabon hills in the early nineteenth century, and in the Welsh language the ponies of North Wales are still referred to as 'merlynnod' or 'merliws'.

Until 1920 the Wynnes of Coed Coch kept only Thoroughbred horses and hunters, and John Jones, the stud groom who was born on the estate in 1875, travelled premium stallions as far afield as Kirkcudbright and Dumfries in Scotland, as well as many other distant counties in England. John Jones was in the employ-ment of three generations of the Wynne family: John Lloyd Wynne, his son Major-Gen. Edward Williams-Wynn, and grandson Edward (Teddy) Wynne. Teddy Wynne was killed in action in September 1916 and the estate passed to his mother (who had re-married), the Hon. Mrs Laurence Brodrick, in trust for his half-sister Margaret (Daisy) Brodrick and kinsman Edward Williams-Wynn. When John Jones died in his 90th year in 1965, still the acting stud groom, it was his proud boast to have served under six 'masters' at Coed Coch.

It was on a Saturday in 1924 when Miss Brodrick and John Jones were returning from hunting that he suggested keeping some Mountain ponies to graze the rough pastures on the highlands of the estate. Miss Brodrick needed no encouragement and soon persuaded her mother what a valuable asset they would be at Coed Coch, although presumably not realising that it was the start of a world-famous venture.

The following Monday Miss Brodrick and John Jones rode over to the parish of Trofarth and bought five mares from Mrs Martha Evans who was a tenant on the estate. And so the Coed Coch Stud started with five wild and unhandled mares, one of which, Coed Coch Gell, producing eight foals at Coed Coch despite being 15 years old when bought.

Later in 1924 the two half-sisters Coed Coch Eirlys and Coed Coch Stretton were acquired from Mr Norton of Lydbury, and Gwenci Mynydd from Captain Howson. Stretton produced nothing of note; Gwenci Mynydd produced Coed Coch Pryfllwyd, a stallion whose influence spread throughout Wales via the many times premium stallion Eryri Gwyndaf, who was a son of Pryfllwyd's daughter, Coed Coch Shonet. By far the greatest influence on the Coed Coch Stud was obtained through Eirlys, who can be regarded as *the* foundation mare of the stud. The first foal from Eirlys was named Coed Coch Seren (responsible for about half of the 136 Section As on the 1978 sale); after 1925 Miss Brodrick named all the families with the same initial letter so the future progeny of Eirlys, which included many good winners, were Ebrill, Eira, Eog and Eurliw Goch. It was Seren who started the stud competing at shows, winning 21 first prizes during the period 1931–7 at major shows including the Royal Welsh, Royal of England and National Pony Shows.

Other notable acquisitions of this period were Gatley Stardust (foaled in 1923), from whom came the Sensigl and Symwl families; Grove Madcap (foaled in 1921), dam of Mefusen who was the dam of Meilyr (Royal Welsh Show male champion in 1950) and the great Madog, who was nine times Royal Welsh male champion between 1951 and 1962; Tanybwlch Prancio (foaled in 1932), dam of Prydferth and Pioden whose descendants include Pelydrog (winner of 65 first prizes and 30 championships), Proffwyd (exported to Lady Creswick, Victoria, Australia in 1961), Pryd (1969 Royal Welsh Show male champion), Pela, Planed (male champion at the 1954 Royal Welsh Show when only two years old); and finally Dinarth Henol (foaled in 1927), who was at Coed Coch for only three years (where she was known as Gwenol) before being sold at the first Coed Coch sale in 1936. The mating of the seven-year-old Henol to the 25-year-old Revolt resulted in Coed Coch Glyndwr being born in 1935. It seems he was a small, weakly foal and if he had not been seen by John Jones's grandson Shem on his way home from school, he might not have survived. Shem carried Glyndwr for over a mile (with Henol following behind) to receive attention at the Home Farm, without knowing that this foal was going to revolutionise Welsh pony breeding throughout the world.

Although 36 ponies were sold on the 1936 sale there were another 34 left and these were offered for sale by auction on 28 August 1937, the catalogue stating that 'for private reasons Miss Brodrick is regretfully compelled to disperse her stud of ponies'. This was a most exciting sale. A Mr S. Walton from Leeds (who had not previously owned any ponies) bought 31 of the Coed Coch ponies, plus another four from other vendors, for which he paid £1,099 (an average of £31). Top price of the sale was 63 guineas paid for Coed Coch Serliw, a four-year-old red roan mare (Revolt x Coed Coch Seren), who had won five first prizes at major shows and was in foal to Glyndwr. Glyndwr himself went to Mr Walton for 45 guineas, as did Coed

*Left to right:* Coed Coch Glyndwr (when owned by the Shalbourne Stud), Miss Brodrick with Coed Coch Siaradus, Shem Jones with Coed Coch Madog, and John Jones with Coed Coch Pwyll.

Coch Sirius (later to become dam of Siaradus, winner of 41 championships including five championships at Royal Welsh Shows) for 14 guineas. It transpired that Mr Walton had no land on which to keep any ponies nor any previous experience with animals, and Miss Brodrick was persuaded to keep the ponies at Coed Coch for a fortnight until a second sale on behalf of Mr Walton could be arranged. At the second sale Miss Brodrick bought Glyndwr back for 30 guineas, along with several others at lower prices than she had sold them to Mr Walton. Serliw came to Ceulan where she remained until her death in 1962. She was female champion at the 1949 Royal Welsh Show and produced many lovely offspring, three of which were exported to the USA. Her 1938 foal Ceulan Revolt was Glyndwr's first foal. He had a big influence on the ponies of Wales, winning many premiums, and his sons, Ceulan Revelry and Ceulan Reveller, were also successful premium stallions. Serliw's daughter to remain at Coed Coch was Seirian, later to become granddam of the famous Madog and a big winner for the Gredington Stud.

Glyndwr stayed on at Coed Coch until 1943 when, with Miss Brodrick abroad as part of her most valuable and untiring contribution to the war effort, he was sold to Lady Wentworth who had been anxious to acquire him for some time. After Miss Brodrick returned from the war and numbers started to increase again at Coed Coch, several mares were sent to Glyndwr every year while he was at Wentworth Stud and in the later ownership of Miss de Beaumont of Shalbourne.

Miss Brodrick was a wonderful ambassador for the Welsh breeds overseas and the post-war exports (such as the nine Section A mares exported to Mrs Charles Illiff of Maryland, USA in 1948) were entirely as a result of her pioneering efforts. When orders were received at Coed Coch, if there were not suitable ponies there, Miss Brodrick would tour Wales with John Jones and her Keeshond dog Jan in her big old-fashioned Hillman car to find them. Of the nine Illiff mares, four were from Coed Coch with another two from Revel and one each from Criban, Ceulan and Gatesheath. One of my childhood treats was to 'skip' school to accompany Miss Brodrick and John Jones on their pony-finding missions in Mid and South Wales. Many a tale can be told of the Hillman car, such as when the steering wheel came off near Aberystwyth and the car ended up on its roof. Miss Brodrick was unscathed but John Jones had to spend some time in hospital.

By 1952 the number of ponies at Coed Coch had increased sufficiently to enable a reduction sale of 50 ponies to be held at the Coed Coch Home Farm on 26 September. The prices realised were average for that period, the 50 ponies selling for £2,315 (average = £46), with Gretton Moonlight, Vean Bog Cotton, Coed Coch

106

Coed Coch Glyndwr when in the ownership of Miss de Beaumont. (*Photo courtesy of Len Davies*)

Mari Las and Downland Butterfly selling to the USA. The Section B mare Coed Coch Pluen (Tanybwlch Berwyn x Tanybwlch Penwen) topped the sale at 135 guineas, having won first prizes at the English Royal and National Pony Shows. Coed Coch Berwynfa, later to become famous as a sire of champion Section B ponies, sold for 45 guineas (as a yearling) but was fortunately bought back for the stud.

For the next few years regular consignments (e.g. 16 in 1955) were sold on the Fayre Oaks Sale, where prices were not spectacular until the big American demand of 1957 when prices increased three- and fourfold.

For health reasons Miss Brodrick was advised to reduce the stud in 1959 and on 26 September 123 ponies were offered for sale at the Home Farm; these included all the Section Bs with the exception of one stallion (Coed Coch Berwynfa) and three mares, leaving some 80 or so Section As to carry on the stud. Some outstanding animals were included on this sale; consequently there was enormous demand for them from home and overseas buyers, and the 123 Coed Coch ponies fetched over £23,000 (average of £187). Star of the sale was the eleven-year-old Section A mare Coed Coch Symwl (Coed Coch Seryddwr x Coed Coch Sensigl). Winner of 37 first prizes and 10 championships, she was secured for £1,200 by Lord Kenyon, for whom she won the Royal Welsh Show Championship the following year. Mrs Mountain of the Twyford Stud paid £945 for Coed Coch Sws, a bay daughter of the famous Siaradus, and Lord Swansea paid £735 for Sws's two-year-old son Coed Coch Siglen Las, who was later to be twice Royal Welsh Male Champion (1965 and

Coed Coch Siglen Las, owned by Lord Swansea, Fourth Baron, from 1959 to 1964. Royal Welsh Show champion 1965 and 1966. (*Photo courtesy of Les Mayall*)

1966). Two high-priced females to be sold for export to Canada were Coed Coch Pwysi (£970 to Mrs F. M. Ross) and Glascoed Tesni (£680 to Mrs Rockwell). Coed Coch Gold Mair, granddam of British and Australian Section B top sire Keston Royal Occasion, sold for £230 (as a foal); her dam Cefn Graceful by Ceulan Revelry sold for £370, also to Canada (Mr Campbell Moodie).

Miss Brodrick always declined praise for her pony breeding enterprise, giving all the credit to John Jones and his family. John Jones was the youngest of 10 children and he himself had 10 children, one son Gordon having been stud groom at Gredington for many years. After John Jones's time, control of the stud fell to his grandson, Shem, assisted by his son Wyn, John Jones Hir (tall John) and John Jones Bach (short John). The respect which Miss Brodrick had for her staff is reflected by the fact that when she went to Buckingham Palace in March 1961 to receive the MBE from the Queen Mother, it was her loyal friend John Jones and his daughter Lil who accompanied her.

Miss Brodrick died suddenly a few days before Christmas in 1962. She had spent most of her lifetime in the Welsh countryside amongst the Welsh people whom she loved so dearly; a kind and cheerful friend with a mission in life to help people in all walks of life. Tanybwlch Berwyn (1924–53) and the elegant Siaradus (1942–62) are both buried in the garden at Plas Llewelyn. The Coed Coch estate passed to Lt. Col. Edward Williams-Wynn who paid the highest tribute to the staff – old John, Shem, Wyn and the two young Johns – for their loyalty and co-operation in the difficult times of re-establishing the stud under new ownership. Continuity was achieved with the least possible disturbance, the breeding policy remained un-altered, and major awards were won throughout Britain. Colonel Edward, though having had no previous experience with Welsh ponies, soon became tremendously enthusiastic. He would attend all the shows and exhibitions himself and obviously had a deep affection for the ponies and a determination to continue the successes achieved by Miss Brodrick over 38 years.

On 27 August 1969 an Open Day was held at Coed Coch as part of Wales's Croeso '69 Celebrations. The parade was led by the 22-year-old Coed Coch Madog followed by his son Salsbri (out of Siaradus) and various other sons and grandsons. Then came the Section A mares in groups: the Coed Coch Seirian group, then Prydferth's, Purwen's and Anwyled's.

Major awards continued to flow into Coed Coch in Colonel Edward's ownership. Pelydrog (granddaughter of the original Tanybwlch Prancio) was female champion at the 1964 Royal Welsh Show and overall champion the following year; Coed Coch

Pryd (grandson of Prancio) was male champion in 1969 and reserve overall to Coed Coch Swyn (great-great-great-granddaughter of the original Eirlys); Coed Coch Glenda (great-granddaughter of the original Gatley Stardust) was female champion in 1973; and Coed Coch Bari, the three-year-old son of Swyn, was overall champion in 1974. Other Royal Welsh Show championships of this period fell to Miss Russell-Allen's Coed Coch Siglen Las, Mr J. Hendy's Coed Coch Norman, Lt. Col. Rosser-John's Treharne Tomboy (son of Coed Coch Blodyn), Mr R. Swain's Ready Token Glen Bride (daughter of Coed Coch Bugail), Sir Harry Llewellyn's Rowfant Prima Ballerina (daughter of Coed Coch Madog), Lord Kenyon's Gred-

Lt. Col. Edward Williams-Wynn OBE, who inherited the Coed Coch estate on the death of Miss Margaret Brodrick in 1962, and continued the stud with great success and devotion until his death in 1977.

110

ington Simwnt (son of Coed Coch Madog and Coed Coch Symwl), Miss Russell-Allen's Dyfrdwy Midnight Moon (daughter of Coed Coch Planed), Mr and Mrs David Reynold's Rondeels Pengwyn (son of Coed Coch Pwffiad) and Mr and Mrs Peter Hicks's Valleylake Breeze (daughter of Coed Coch Glynlws).

And so it is obvious that the Coed Coch Stud was continuing in all its former glory under the guidance of Lt. Col. Edward Williams-Wynn, and it was a great shock to Welsh pony breeders throughout the world to learn of his sudden death on 8 September 1977. Lt. Col. Edward Watkin Williams-Wynn, OBE, was a quiet man, immensely kind and with a wonderful dry sense of humour. With no previous experience of Welsh pony breeding when he took over the stud in 1962, he soon got to know the names and pedigrees of the 200 or so ponies at the stud. He served as a very valuable member of the WPCS Council and was president for 1974–5. With his death the staff at Coed Coch felt as if the bottom had dropped out of their world, and despite many efforts to try to save the stud, e.g. to be run on a smaller scale at the University College of North Wales, there was no solution other than to offer the 244 ponies for sale on 7 September 1978. The stud staff were given a mare of their own choosing and permanent homes were found for all the mares over 16 years old.

The weather on 7 September 1978 was not too kind but it failed to dampen the enthusiasm of the hundreds of Welsh pony breeders who had come from the four corners of the globe to try to secure an animal which it had taken 54 years of dedicated and selective breeding to produce. The 120 Section As (despite 36 of them being foals) returned the fantastic average figure of £1,055, boosted by the world record figure of 21,000 guineas (equivalent to double this figure today) paid by Lady Creswick of Victoria, Australia (with Lord Kenyon as under-bidder) for the seven-year-old former Royal Welsh Show champion Coed Coch Bari, and 14,000 guineas paid by Mrs Doris Gadsden of the Bengad Stud for his 15-year-old full brother Coed Coch Saled. Top Section A female was Coed Coch Tarian, daughter of Saled out of Mari (daughter of Anwyled), for which the Countess of Dysart paid 4,200 guineas. Coed Coch Helen, a five-year-old daughter of Salsbri and another Anwyled daughter, Anwen, was bought for 3,000 guineas by Mr and Mrs Harry Fetherstonhaugh, who inherited the Coed Coch estate and are continuing breeding ponies from Coed Coch bloodlines under the 'Bryndansi' prefix.

The sale total of £184,453, representing the wonderful average of £842, reflected the value which breeders placed on 54 years of devotion of two gifted breeders. The last pony to bear the Coed Coch prefix was sale lot 175, a colt foal named Coed

Coed Coch Saled selling for 14,000 guineas at the Coed Coch dispersal sale on 7 September 1978. (*Photo courtesy of Margaret Salisbury ARPS*)

Coch Pen-y-Daith which is Welsh for 'End-of-Journey'. So the prefix no longer exists but its influence will continue for many decades.

## The Revel Stud

It was in 1895 that John Griffiths moved to live at the Revel Farm in the parish of Talgarth in the old county of Brecknock (present county of Powys). The name of the farm, The Revel, is an anglicised version of the Welsh word 'Yr Efail', the Blacksmith's Forge. The farmhouse and adjoining buildings, with pastures and arable land around it, lie at the bottom of the Breconshire Black Mountains, near the village of Cwmdu (Black Valley), and since the land borders on to the Black Mountains there are grazing rights, shared with all other farmers (some of them 20 miles away) whose own lands border the Black Mountains.

Originally Mr Griffiths kept Cobs at the Revel, e.g. Revel Nell, foaled in 1928, a daughter of Welsh Model (foaled in 1910) by Caradog Flyer (foaled in 1896). Some Mountain ponies were also acquired in the 1920s, mainly from the nearby studs of 'Criban' (H. W. Richards and Sons) and 'Forest' (W. S. Miller of Forest Lodge). Typical of the purchases of that time are the stallion Revel Grey (foaled in 1922, bred at Criban by Bwlch Quicksilver out of Criban White Flash), and the mares Revel Greylight (foaled in 1928, bred at Forest by Forest Black Lad out of Forest Sweeps Stamp) and Forest Black Style, foaled in 1922. When John Griffiths died in 1944, his son Emrys inherited the farm, and Emrys and his wife Dinah have become world-famous for their Welsh ponies.

However, while much of the credit for the breeding and showring successes of Revel ponies is due to the more recent acquisitions of Mr and Mrs Emrys Griffiths, we must not forget many outstanding successes for the Revel Stud (and many others) emanating from the foundations laid by the late John Griffiths. Take as examples two Royal Welsh Show champions: Revel Springsong (foaled in 1950), champion of the 1957 Royal Welsh Show, was out of Revel Serenade (foaled in 1940), out of Revel Cuckoo (foaled in 1934), out of Revel Light Grey (foaled in 1931), out of Revel Greylight (above); and Revel Jewel (foaled in 1954), champion of the 1962 Royal Welsh Show, was out of Revel Jean (foaled in 1949), out of Revel Judy (foaled in 1934), out of Revel Bay Leaf (foaled in 1931), by Revel Grey (above) out of Forest Black Style (above).

The effect of these original mares on other studs can be appreciated by considering Baledon Verity (foaled in 1979), female champion at the 1989 Royal Welsh Show. Her sire is Revel Janus, son of Revel Jade who is a daughter of the same Revel Jean. On her dam's side Baledon Verity is indebted to another 'early' mare with the rather ignominious name of Grwyne Sack! Grwyne Sack, daughter of Revel Blue Stone, was foaled in 1934, and in 1941 she produced Revel Vintage, dam of Revel Viza (foaled 1958), dam of Revel Vienna (foaled in 1962), dam of Revel Venetia (foaled in 1967), who has produced a whole host of well-known Baledon ponies including Baledon Verity. Another influential mare was Pretty Girl

The Revel Farm. Birthplace of Mr Emrys Griffiths and of 175 Welsh Mountain pony stallions and 458 mares in the ten years 1957–66. (*Photo: Wynne Davies*)

(foaled in 1922), bred by Harvey N. Jones of Irfon Marvel fame. Pretty Girl's daughter by Revel Chief was Revel Dawn (foaled in 1933), and her son (foaled in 1942, sired by Llwyn Tom Tit) was Revel Revolt. There are not many current Revel ponies who do not have one (or more) strains of Revel Revolt in their pedigrees.

Another Forest-bred 'Revel' mare was Revel Forest Bay (foaled in 1921). Her daughter was Revel Dazzle (foaled in 1942), whose daughter Revel Seren (foaled in 1945) by the influential Criban Grey Grit was herself dam of Revel Siren (foaled in 1958). Siren is well represented throughout Wales via her daughters Revel Sybil (Menai Stud) and Revel Siesta (foaled in 1961), who had only one foal in Britain (Ceulan Sprite, foaled in 1964) before she was exported to South Africa.

The next major influx to the Revel occurred in 1943 when the mares Winestead Larina, Winestead Zenia and Winestead Teresa and the foundation stock mares Revel Bay Lass, Revel Daybreak, Revel Fair Lady (Weston Stud) and Revel Mysteria were purchased from William Hay of Winestead Hall, Patrington, East

Yorkshire. Winestead Larina (foaled 1932) was a daughter of Grove Star of Hope, one of the most beautiful mares ever to grace the Welsh Stud Book. At the Revel, Winestead Larina produced Revel Springlight (1942), the 1959 Royal Welsh Show champion Revel Rosette (1948, sired by Revel Revolt), Revel Light (1950), who ended his days at Ceulan, and Revel Lady (1951). I was actually staying at the Revel on one of my university holidays, several of which I spent enjoying the wonderful hospitality of Dinah and Emrys Griffiths and surrounded by these superb ponies in their exquisite natural surroundings, when Winestead Larina decided she had had a good life and passed away peacefully on 2 July 1952. Winestead Teresa, daughter of Larina, produced the good premium stallion Revel Ballet Dancer (1943), Dewdrop (1944), Blue Boy (1946) and Churchill (Coedowen Stud, 1949).

Mr Emrys Griffiths with Revel Rosette (foaled in 1948 by Revel Revolt x Winestead Larina), champion at the 1959 Royal Welsh Show. (*Photo: Wynne Davies*)

Winestead Zenia, foaled the same year as Larina, was a daughter of Ness Thistle, the 'full back' of George Lyell's show string of the 1920s. Ness Thistle was sired by the invincible Bleddfa Shooting Star during the time (1914) when he was leased to Dafydd Evans's Llwyncadfor Stud in South Cardiganshire. Thistle was bred by Evan Jones, the blacksmith of Caerwedros, out of Wedros Gem by the pony of Cob-type stallion, Eiddwen Flyer III, granddam Wedros Bell by King Flyer (15 hands 1 in.). Despite her Cob background, the progeny of Zenia verged on the 'elegant', proving again how interdependent the four Welsh sections have been during their development. The best known of Winestead Zenia's progeny was Revel Playtime (foaled in 1950), sired by Pendock Playboy. Playtime deserves her place amongst the most influential of all females ever at the Revel. One daughter of Playtime was Revel Pinup (by Revel Light), foaled in 1953 and recipient of the championship trophy from HM The Queen at the Brecon Bicentenary Show in 1956. Two mares of this family which were at Ceulan for a long time are Revel Piquante (Brierwood Goldleaf x Pinup), foaled in 1964 and died in 1989, and Revel Phillipa (foaled in 1971), sired by Revel Chip out of Playtime. These families have had a great influence in many overseas countries. Vardra Julius (Twyford Sprig x Revel Pinup) was one of the top sires in Holland and came back to spend a season in Wales (1988); Revel Playsome (Twyford Sprig x Revel Playtime) was a champion in Belgium who then went to Australia, where he continued to be many-times champion and top sire; and Revel Pye (Clan Pip x Revel Pinup) was leading sire at Brierwood and Weston before he too went to Australia.

Reference has already been made to Pendock Playboy, the bay colt foaled in 1947 and sired by Bowdler Blueboy out of Craven Tosca. Playboy was sold to the Revel where he died as a two-year-old in 1949 after covering only four mares. The mating to four mares had such an enormous effect on the Welsh Mountain pony breed as a whole that one wonders what his influence would have been had he lived a normal span of years. Three of his progeny have already been described: Revel Light out of Winestead Larina; Revel Playtime out of Winestead Zenia; and Revel Springsong, champion of the 1957 Royal Welsh Show and daughter of Revel Serenade, a beautiful palomino mare which was sold to Miss Hetty Mackay-Smith of the USA but died shortly afterwards, after producing a filly foal. The fourth of his progeny was Revel Fun (FS2), a dun daughter of Revel Fair Lady whose other daughter was Revel Fair Maid (Weston Stud). An inbred 'Pendock Playboy' was Revel Frolic (foaled in 1953), by Revel Light out of Revel Fun. Vardra Julius combines three Pendock Playboy strains: his sire, Twyford Sprig, is a son of

116

Springsong, and his dam, Revel Pinup, is a daughter of Revel Light and Revel Playtime.

The next milestone in the history of the Revel was probably the Vardra dispersal sale held at Gowerton market on 16 April 1951, Mr Matthew Williams of the Vardra Stud having died on 26 January 1951. Lots 7 and 8 were two fillies foaled in 1949, both sired by Vardra Sunstar (Criban Pebble x 1947 Royal Welsh Show champion Vardra Charm). He was a useful dark grey stallion who stood second to Coed Coch Madog at the 1951 Royal Welsh Show when owned by Criban Stud, after which he was sold to the USA. Mr Emrys Griffiths bought both lots (for 33 gns and 11 gns), and one wonders if he suspected that he was buying two future Royal Welsh Show champions that day. The smaller one, registered as Revel Choice, was female champion at the 1961 Royal Welsh Show, and her daughter, Revel Caress (by Revel Springlight, son of Winestead Larina), was overall champion at the 1963 show. The larger one was registered as Revel Nance and she was Section B champion at the 1951 Royal Welsh Show. Choice, apart from making a name in the showring, perhaps more importantly left an indelible mark on the breed through her progeny, which include: Chancellor and Crusader (two very sought-after sires); Cascade, Caress and Copelia, three top mares; Consul, who was exported to New Zealand where he was a very popular sire; Courtier (Vishon Stud); Capri, a good producer at the Revel; then five foals by Clan Pip from 1963 to 1967: Chip (Quinton and Penhasset Studs), Cello (Bengad Stud), Chase (Persie Stud), Cassino (winner of 270 championships including male championship at the 1976 Royal Welsh Show and overall champion in 1977 for Hollybush Stud), Chelsea, a wonderful producer at the Revel; and finally Choosey by Twyford Sprig.

I remember my father remarking after a visit to the Revel in 1961 that he had seen the best Mountain pony two-year-old ever that day, and he had been viewing ponies over 46 years! This was Clan Pip (Clan Tony x Clan Prue). After the death of his breeder, Mr Arthur McNaught, the Revel became home for him and five other stallions (Clan Dave, Clan Dirk, Clan Dash, Clan Gylen and Clan Gille), and also some Clan mares including the 1966 and 1967 Royal Welsh overall champion Clan Peggy and her dam Clan Prue. The most famous of all these is undoubtedly Clan Pip, his most recent prizewinning son being Jill and Stuart Abrahall's Flydon Henri-ap-Pip born within a few days of the death of his sire in 1981. Another very successful Clan Pip grandson was Revel Japhet (Revel Chip x Clan Jill), who was Royal Welsh champion in 1982 and overall champion in 1984 and 1986 for the Menai Stud.

Mr Emrys Griffiths with Revel Jewel (Revel Hailstone x Revel Jean), champion at the 1962 Royal Welsh Show. (*Photo: Wynne Davies*)

Not many other bloodlines have been added to the Revel in recent years, one worthy exception being Rhydyfelin Seren Heulyn (foaled in 1959), granddam of Revel Hetty who produced (in 1982, sired by Cantref Glory) Waxwing Herod, who was overall champion at the 1983 RASE Show, Lloyds Bank qualifier over all in-hand breeds, and now sire of top-selling stock in Australia.

In 1985 Mr and Mrs Griffiths decided to take things easier and moved to the adjoining smaller Glan Nant farm. However, they still seem to be as busy as ever and champions (e.g. 1990 International Show supreme champion Revel Hibiscus) are produced from Glan Nant just the same as they were from Revel. The world-wide influence of the Revel Stud is appreciated when one realises that Revel ponies

118

form the highest percentage within the WPCS in Holland, and the league table of imports into Australia recorded in their Stud Book Volume 3 (1980) reads as follows: Coed Coch (13, mainly from the dispersal sale), Weston (12), Twyford (11), Crossways (9), Revel (6), followed by exports from another 12 British studs.

# 6 The Welsh Mountain pony today

Since 1950, when numbers of Welsh Mountain ponies became reasonably secure after the ravages of war, Section A of the Welsh Stud Book has been self-contained and consequently their type has become much more stabilised. Up until 1950, animals of Section B and C breeding which failed to grow over 12 hands could be registered in Section A, often leading to very diverse types in future generations. To be eligible for registration in Section A of the Welsh Stud Book today, both parents must be registered within the section and foals must be registered in the year of their birth.

Of the 6,000 or so animals registered annually in the Welsh Stud Book in the

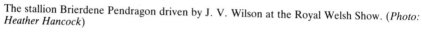
The stallion Brierdene Pendragon driven by J. V. Wilson at the Royal Welsh Show. (*Photo: Heather Hancock*)

120

Leading-rein pony Bengad Pernettya, a daughter of Bengad Nepeta who is a very successful sire of leading-rein ponies. (*Photo: Pleasure Prints*)

early 1990s, about 2,000 each are Sections A and D, followed by 800 Section Bs, 700 Welsh part-breds and 500 Section Cs. The large numbers of Welsh Mountain ponies bred and registered annually are an indication of their popularity and reflect the demand for them.

Why, therefore, is the Welsh Mountain pony so popular and to what uses can it be put? The Welsh Mountain pony for many years has been recognised as the most beautiful pony in the world and some are kept and bred purely to give the owner satisfaction to look at and admire something beautiful, coupled with very little cost of keeping and minimal problems or veterinary care. Welsh Mountain ponies are also famous for their kind temperament. Showing Welsh Mountain ponies in hand has become a very popular hobby, often with exhibitors who have had immense experience with larger horses (e.g. hunters), but who have decided to lead an easier life in later years. There were 429 Welsh Mountain ponies entered in the in-hand classes at the 1991 Royal Welsh Show, the largest class (yearling fillies) containing 61 entries. The ultimate aim of every Welsh Mountain pony breeder is to win the coveted 'Captain Howson Memorial trophy' awarded to the champion in-hand exhibit at the Royal Welsh Show.

When showing a Welsh Mountain pony in hand it is important to keep the 'native' image. By all means make certain that the pony is clean, trim off any unsightly whiskers under the chin or protruding from the ears, and train the mane so that it falls flat on the offside. If the top of the tail is bushy it can be thinned out with a comb, which will give the image of stronger hind-quarters when viewed from behind. What looks out of place on native ponies is an excess of make-up, e.g. eye shadow and black, shiny hoof oil. The bridle should be neat and fitting well; white halters are often sufficient for youngstock or mares.

Ponies should be taught to trot out well at home. A pony which pulls back will often move wide behind and not look happy in his work. All ponies should walk smartly with a good stride; Welsh Mountain ponies are noted for a long stride at the trot, and all joints should be well flexed with plenty of freedom from the shoulder. Ponies with upright shoulders will not have this freedom of movement and stallions with upright shoulders should be avoided. When viewed from the front or behind, it is important that the legs move in a straight line without 'dishing' in front or bent hocks behind.

In recent years too much emphasis has been placed on having minute ears, large bulging eyes and short squeezed-up heads, with insufficient attention being paid to more important aspects of conformation, with the result that this type of head is often accompanied by upright shoulders, short thick necks and low-set tails. This is not the type which lends itself to performance (i.e. riding or driving) and consequently more attention is now being placed on 'performance' conformation.

Welsh Mountain ponies usually constitute the major winners among children's riding ponies in the 'leading-rein' and 'first-ridden' categories. Part-bred Section A ponies usually hold their own in the 12 hands 2 in. and 13 hands 2 in. show riding pony classes and working hunter pony competitions, where the cunning performance aptitude, developed over many centuries of living on the Welsh hills, stands them in good stead when it comes to the jumping phase.

Welsh Mountain ponies have developed over the years true-to-type on the high

Brierwood Rocket, champion Welsh Mountain pony at the Royal Welsh Show in 1985 and 1988. (*Photo: Carol Gilson Photography*)

and sparse hills of Wales. When bred in 'artificial' surroundings, for example the lush grasslands of the Vale of Glamorgan, the English Home Counties or overseas, it is essential that they not be allowed to get too fat, otherwise they will develop laminitis and mares will be difficult to get in foal.

Adult ponies should be able to thrive in winter given only good hay and clean water. A shelter from driving rain will help prevent 'weather beat'. Foals will benefit in later life if they are given some concentrated food during their first winter, and a shelter from the rain is essential, though foals will often prefer to be

Mr Jack Havard driving Mr G. C. Smith's Whatton Penaeth (sire of three-times Royal Welsh Show champion Aston Superstar) to win the harness class at the 1971 Royal Welsh Show.

out in snow than in their shelter if given free access. Foals which are required to have lost their winter coats in time for early shows are often stabled permanently from the time of weaning.

Also since the time of Julius Caesar it has been recognised that the Welsh Mountain pony is a first-rate little trapper, often to be seen pulling a smart gig or governess cart in private driving competitions, or high-stepping away in a 'show-waggon'; performances in which adults can participate. Perhaps nowadays the virtues of the Welsh Mountain pony as a harness pony is more greatly appreciated overseas than in its native surroundings, very large numbers appearing, driven by children and adults, in Holland, Denmark, South Africa etc.

# Bibliography

Dargan, Olive Tilford. *The Welsh Pony*. Charles A. Stone, Boston, USA, 1913 (private printing)

Davies, Wynne. *Welsh Ponies and Cobs*. J. A. Allen, 1980; 2nd edn 1985

Davies, Wynne. *Welsh Champions*. J. A. Allen, 1984

Hulme, Susan. *Native Ponies of the British Isles*. Saiga, 1980

Wentworth, Lady. *Horses and Ponies of Britain*. Collins, 1944

Welsh Stud Books, volume 1 (1902) to present

Welsh Pony and Cob Society Journals, 1962 to present

# Index of ponies' names

Page numbers in italics refer to illustrations